Quilt-Inspired Designs in Split Ring Tatting

KAREN BOVARD © 2015

Published by: The ShuttleSmith Publishing Company
9102 Poppleton Avenue
Omaha, Nebraska 68124   USA

www.TheShuttleSmith.com

theshuttlesmith@gmail.com
k.bovard@yahoo.com

ISBN: 978-0-9835441-3-5

Other books by Karen Bovard / The ShuttleSmith Publishing Company

Fun with Split Ring Tatting

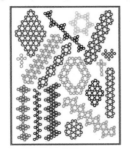

Karen Bovard

MORE Fun with Split Ring Tatting

Karen Bovard

BLOCK ALPHABETS IN SPLIT RING TATTING

Karen Bovard

Patchwork Quilt Designs in Split Ring Tatting

Karen Bovard

INTRODUCTION   I have finally found a way to study and enjoy quilts and quilting without diving into the world of fabrics, sewing/quilting machines, & all the other gizmos and gadgets that go with a new/different artform. I have long admired quilting and have always said "Someday I'm going to do that". But so far that time has not come....I'm too busy with the artform that I love--tatting. All that changed when I decided that I could create my own inperpretation of quilting in the form of tatting. Split Ring Tatting Technique provided me with the perfect *(in my mind!)* medium.

This foray into studying quilting and creating tatting designs was an enjoyable one. Quilting (like tatting) is based upon repetition and symmetry--both concepts that I find soothing in what can seem like a chaotic world. Quilting however, can allow us tatters to venture into a new world...that of COLOR. Never before have we as tatters had so many luscious colors of thread to choose from as that supplied by Handy Hands in their LizBeth thread line. At the time of this writing, there were over 160 colors in the many sizes of thread that tatters use. It seems to me that those thread colors were just waiting for a book of designs such as supplied by quilt-inspired patterns. The variegated threads even mimic printed fabric. I have been tatting for several decades and I have never really had such an opportunity to play with and put together multiple colors in one design. I am still a novice with color....some of my combinations I like others could be better. But I am having fun with color.

Follow Karen Bovard on her blog & website at:
www.TheShuttleSmith.com

Karen is available to teach a variety of tatting & other lacemaking techniques.

Check out some ideas at: http://theshuttlesmithclasses.blogspot.com/

Let Karen custom-design a class for your group that is guaranteed to challenge or just be fun.

This book is a compilation of designs that I came up with that are outside the norm of what is featured in my other Quilt-Inspired book titled *Patchwork Quilt Blocks in Split Ring Tatting.* All the patterns are created using only rings--regular, split or take-off rings. There are NO chains.

The designs are based upon the basic elements/shapes of historical quilt blocks such as 'Log Cabin', 'Grandmothers Flower Garden', & 'Flying Geese'. These designs feature more open-work grounds & exploration of designs based upon diamonds and hexagons. The designs are more irregular in size and shape.

24 additional illustrations are provided as 'Future Designs', 'Design Ideas', and 'Color Options'.

Unfortunately not all the blocks have tatted-thread pieces done. I just don't have the time to tat all my designs anymore--sure wish I did!

Many thanks to Barbara Foster at Handy Hands for donating many balls of LizBeth thread to this project. There are soooo many colors to choose from, that it was quite a delemma choosing what I wanted to use.

Once again another big 'Thank You' to my friend, Jennifer Bartling, for dropping everything to proof-read the patterns on my 'I need it now!' schedule.

TABLE OF CONTENTS / PATTERNS

Karen Bovard/The ShuttleSmith demoing tatting at a Quilt Show

Karen Bovard is an empty-nester, newly-married tatter who lives in Omaha, Nebraska where she works full-time in a medical laboratory. When not tatting, she enjoys riding motorcycles & would love the chance to travel via motorcycle to teach at &/or attend tatting/lacemaking workshops.

Note: No tattoos, piercing or leather involved.

GUIDE/KEY TO *THE SHUTTLESMITH'S* VISUAL PATTERNS

The Following Standard Abbreviations are Used

R	=	**Ring**
SR	=	**Split Ring**
TOR	=	**Take Off Ring/Thrown Off Ring**

As in all Visual/Illustrated Patterns

- The first ring tatted that has a picot is when you will tat that picot.
- The ensuing ring tatted that is associated with that same picot will be a join

Key Points of Illustrated/Visual Patterns

Color of Portions/Arcs
- Each color represents one of two shuttle/thread sources.

Direction of the Arcs (from Dots to Arrowhead)
- Shows which way regular rings & the portions of split rings are worked.
- Gives direction as to how the ring is to be tatted if Frontside/Backside Tatting Technique is used.
- Gives direction as to when the work is to be reversed.

Colored Letters
- Dictate which portion of a split ring is to be tatted first ('A') with regular, transferred double stitches & then the ('B') portion with untransferred, reverse-stitch double stitches.
- If a split ring does not have join or a TOR associated with it, the portions of the split ring can be tatted in any order *(colored letters will not be indicated)*.

Numbered Rings
- All the rings (regular, take off, or split ring) are numbered sequentially. The path the pattern is to be worked is to start at 'R1' & work in ascending order.

Regular Rings in Visual Patterns--Including Take Off Rings

- The <u>dot</u> designates the starting point of the ring ●
- The <u>arrowhead</u> designates the ending point of the ring. ◀ *(A regular ring starts & ends at the same point.)*
- '**R**' is used to designate a (regular) ring.
- The larger '#'/number (after the 'R') designates the order in which the rings are tatted & thus how the pattern is worked.
- The smaller '#'/number on the inside of the arc is the number of double stitches in the ring or in that particular portion of the ring between picots and joins.

    <u>A regular-tatted ring in Visual Pattern style is distinguised by the fact that</u>:
- There is only 1 arc.
- There is only 1 color used for the arc, starting dot, & ending arrowhead.
- The starting point & the ending point are at the same place on the ring.

Split Rings in Visual Patterns

- 2 <u>dots</u> of different colors designate the starting points of the 2 different thread sources of the split ring. ●●
- 2 <u>arrowheads</u> of different colors designate the ending points of the 2 thread sources of the split ring.
  (A split ring starts & ends at different points.) ▶◀
- The arcs represent the two thread sources that create split rings.
  (When you see a ring diagram with 2 colors used, you know that it is a split ring.)
- The abbreviations '**SR**' are used: the '**S**' meaning 'Split' & the '**R**' meaning 'Ring'.
- The larger '#'/number (after the 'R') designates the order in which the rings are tatted and thus how the pattern is worked.
- The '#'/number on the inside of the arcs is the number of double stitches in the ring or in that particular portion of the ring between picots & joins.

Numbered Rings--Path of the Pattern

- How the pattern is worked (or the 'path') is designated in Visual Patterns by the number inside the rings next to either **R**, **SR**, or **TOR**.
- Start at R1 and then progress numerically (1 then 2, then 3, then 4.....) through the pattern.
- There may be different ways or paths to take to tat the pattern other than the one illustrated. However, the patterns have been carefully designed & charted to lessen the complexity of the pattern & to allow for the following conditions:
  - The pattern can be worked continuously, from start to end, in one round or as few rounds as possible.
  - Regular joins *(not Split Ring Joining Technique)* can be used.
    - Regular joins can only be made on the ***first*** portion of a split ring *(the regular, transferred double stitches)*.
  - Take off rings (TOR's) can be created without the need for an additional thread source.
    - TOR's are created on the ***second*** portion of the split ring *(the untransferred, reverse-stitch double stitches)*.
    - TOR's *(which are regular rings)* allow regular joins to be used.
  - Regular rings are used as often as possible.

-- Some of the split rings in the visual patterns will have colored letter designations (*inside the ring, and next to the stitch count*) and some will not.
-- If a split ring does not have a join or take off ring associated with it, the portions of the split ring can be tatted in any order.

This split ring pattern can be tatted in one of two ways--either choice appropriate:
1. The 12-stitch (green) portion can be tatted first with regular, transferred stitches and then the 4-stitch (red) portion is tatted with reverse, untransferred double stitches.   **OR**
2. Tat the 4-stitch (red) portion first with regular, transferred stitches and then the 12-stitch (green) portion is tatted with reverse, untransferred stitches.

However, the order in which the split ring portions are tatted in some split rings is important for two reasons:
1. To create joins utilizing traditonal tatting joining technique--NOT Split Ring Joining Technique *(which is more cumbersome to master and does not create as 'neat' a join).*
   -- Done from the ***first portion*** (the regular, transferred double stitches)
2. To be able to create Take-Off Rings (TOR's) without the need to use a third thread source.
   -- Done from the ***second portion*** (the reverse, untransferred double stitches)

This split ring pattern dictates that the 12-stitch (green) be tatted first with regular, transferred stitches and then the 4-stitch (red) portion is tatted with reverse, untransferred double stitches.

Just like in the alphabet, 'A' comes before 'B' and thus the 'A' portion is done first.

-- Shows the direction that the ring is worked.
-- Shows which way regular rings and the portions of split rings are worked.
-- Gives clues/direction to how the ring is to be tatted if Frontside/Backside Tatting technique is used.
   -- If the arc of a regular ring is '***clockwise***' then the ring is tatted as a '***frontside***' ring.
   -- If the arc of a regular ring is '***counter-clockwise***' then the ring is tatted as a '***backside***' ring.

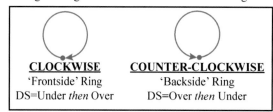

CLOCKWISE
'Frontside' Ring
DS=Under *then* Over

COUNTER-CLOCKWISE
'Backside' Ring
DS=Over *then* Under

In split rings, both clockwise and counter-clockwise arcs/portions are part of each split ring.

The direction of the first portion of the split ring made dictates whether the split ring is tatted as either a 'frontside' or a 'backside' ring.
-If Portion A is '***clockwise***' then the split ring is tatted as a '***frontside***' ring
-If Portion A is '***counter-clockwise***' then the the split ring is tatted as a '***backside***' ring

CLOCKWISE First
'Frontside' Ring
With the 'Red' shuttle make 12 regular, transferred double stitches: ***Under-Stitch-first; followed by Over Stitch***

With the 'Green' shuttle make 4 reverse, untransferred
double stitches: ***Over Stitch-first; followed by Under Stitch***

COUNTER-CLOCKWISE First
'Backside' Ring
With the 'Red' shuttle make 12 regular, transferred double stitches: ***Over-Stitch-first; followed by Under Stitch***

With the 'Green' shuttle make 4 reverse, untransferred
double stitches: ***Under Stitch-first; followed by Over Stitch***

-- Gives visual clues/direction as to when the work is to be reversed. *(Illustrated patterns do NOT give written directions as to when to Reverse Work.)*

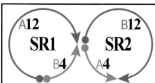

If you tat one ring as a 'frontside' element *(the first portion of the split ring &/or the regular ring is a clockwise arc--**SR1**)* and then the second ring is a 'backside' element *(the first portion of the split ring &/or the regular ring is a counter-clockwise arc--**SR2**)* you will need to Reverse Work between these two rings.

Take Off/Thrown Off Rings (TOR)

-A Take Off/Thrown Off Ring is a 'regular' ring that is created/tatted in the middle of another element. In traditional tatting (rings/chains/no split rings) a Take Off Ring would have been referred to as a 'second-shuttle element' because is was tatted in the middle of a chain element & necessitated the use of a second shuttle. In the case of the patterns in this book, it is made in steps while tatting a Split Ring.

-Take Off Rings allow rings to be tatted that otherwise would have been unable to be tatted/'orphaned'.

-Take Off Rings can be done from either portion of the split ring. If they arise from the first/transferred double stitch portion of the split ring, the thread source to tat the Take Off Ring must come from a third shuttle/thread source & be carried along the ring thread inside the double stitches *(known as Padded Tatting Technique)*. Take Off Rings can be made, without the need for a third thread source, if they are made from the second, untransferred stitch portion of the split ring.

-The patterns in this book were carefully charted so that if you follow the path/plan of the pattern, tatting the split ring portions in the order they are illustrated--*colored A's & B's*, you can tat Take Off Rings using only two thread sources.

-Take Off Rings are tatted as a 'unit', in steps with the split ring it is associated with.

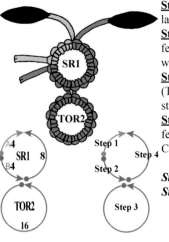

A TOR is tatted as a 'unit', in steps, with the SR it is associated with:

Step 1 With Shuttle A form a ring & make 4 regular, transferred double stitches.

Step 2 With Shuttle B make 4 reverse, untransferred double stitches on the ring thread. Reverse work.

Step 3 With Shuttle B--tat Take Off Ring 2 (TOR2): make 16 regular, transferred double stitches. Close TOR2. Reverse work.

Step 4 With Shuttle B make 8 reverse, untransferred double stitches on the ring thread. Close Split Ring 1 by pulling Shuttle A thread.

Steps 1, 2, & 4 create the split ring.
Step 3 creates the take off ring.

More than one Take Off Ring can be make from a single split ring.

This illustration shows a split ring (#2) with 3 Take Off Rings (#3, 4, 5). Rings #1 & 6 are tatted as regular rings.

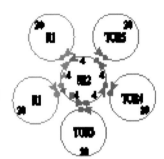

All the Rings in this Book are Designed to be Round-Shaped

-Close the ring by pulling the working shuttle/thread downward, away from the base of the ring.
-Use your fingers to push the ring into a round-shape.

All Rings are Tatted with No-Space of Thread Between Rings

-The visual effect of the pieces in this book is that each ring is closely adjacent to its neighboring ring(s).
-All rings are started as close to one another as possible. NO 'gaposis'!!!

Picot Size--Use of Joining Picots

-The pieces were designed with the idea that all the rings lie in close relationship with one another.
-The picots used in this book/style of tatting are all examples of Joining Picots.
-Joining picots are minute picots that barely allow for insertion of a tiny crochet hook. They are used only for joining, not as ornamental picots. A Joining Picot is barely recognizable as a picot loop.
-A space of thread between the two double stitches that is creating the properly-sized Joining Picot is equal to one double stitch width.
-In the process of facilitating very tight joins between rings, very small joining picots are created. A small-gauge crochet hook is necessary to facilitate these joins.
-Proper Joining Picot size is actually so small that at times it maybe dificult to get even a tiny crochet hook into the picot loop to use it. At these times, a dental-pick tool or a blunt-tipped sewing needle *(such as a Tapestry needle--ca. Size 20, 22, or 24)* is useful to pull the picots out to a sufficient size to be able to insert a joining hook to facilitate the join.
-If you forgot to create a picot, all hope is not lost! Just insert your crochet hook or pick/needle between the stitches where the picot 'should be'. Pull out this horizontal space of thread and use it as a picot. Picots formed this way will be an appropriate size for joining the patterns tatted in this book.

Frontside/Backside Joining Technique

Because these Quilt-Inspired Designs in Split Ring Tatting utilize tatted blocks in different colors, use of Frontside/Backside (FS/BS) Joining Technique is encouraged even if you choose not to use FS/BS Tatting Technique.

The act of making a regular *(sliding, not locking)* join adds an extra horizontal thread to the stitches being tatted. This horizontal thread is the picot you are joining to. If the joining picot is a different color than the ring element you are joining to, then this horizontal thread will show as a 'bleb' of color. It must be managed with Joining Technique/Strategy to not be visually distracting.

Even if you choose not to practice/use Frontside/Backside Tatting Technique, you will need to choose one side of your work to be the backside. By choosing which Joining Technique to use (**Up Join** or **Down Join**) you can manipulate all the horizontal thread spaces of a join to show on one side *(the 'backside')* of the work. This is mainly only important when joining different colored rings together *(such as between the different blocks that make up a quilt block or when utilizing variegated thread within a single block.)*

There are two joining techniques. Both techniques join two elements together. How and when they are used can produce different visual effects due to where the extra horizontal thread (from the picot) ends up--either on the front or backside of the elements.

'Backside' view: You can see the red joining picots in the yellow round & the yellow joining picots in the blue round.

5

Up Join

This is what is regarded as the Traditional Join.

How to work: --Lay the picot **on top** of the working thread of the ring you are joining together.
          --The working thread is brought **UP** and through the picot, the shuttle passed through the loop of thread formed, and the join nestled/tensioned down into position.

The result: The horizontal thread (supplied by the picot) is on the **backside** of the work.

This join is sometimes called a 'Frontside Join' because the horizontal space of thread is toward the 'backside' of the piece/element and does not distract from the 'frontside' of the work. In other words, the 'frontside' is visually preserved.

Down Join

This is a relatively new joining technique.

How to work: --Lay the picot **below** the working thread of the ring you are joining together.
          --The working thread is brought **DOWN** and through the picot, the shuttle passed through the loop of thread formed, and the join nestled/tensioned down into position.

The result: The horizontal thread (supplied by the picot) is on the **frontside** of the work.

SIMPLIFICATION OF **WHICH** JOIN TO USE

Remembering which join (Up vs Down) to use can be daunting. So I have come up with this mental/physical approach to Frontside/Backside Joining Technique.

First: You must decide which side will be your frontside vs. backside....then stick to this plan.

- Lay the working thread on the 'backside' of the joining picot.
- Insert the crochet hook/joining device in the 'frontside' of the picot
- Bring the loop of working thread to the 'frontside' of the piece and insert shuttle through this loop to capture the join, tensioning the join as ususal.

The key point to remember is: Always insert the crochet hook/joining device into the 'frontside' of the picot then bring the loop of thread toward the 'frontside' of the work = you will position the horizontal space of thread to the 'backside' of the piece.

STEP BY STEP INSTRUCTIONS AS TO HOW TO READ *THE SHUTTLESMITH'S* VISUAL PATTERNS

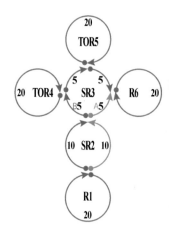

Ring 1 is a regularly-tatted ring. Only one shuttle/thread source is needed. Tat 20 regular, transferred double stitches and then close the ring.

The next ring in Split Ring 2 (SR2). It is an example of an 'even' split ring. To tat this ring, you will need a second shuttle/thread source. Since no colored letters are used in this illustration, either portion (the green or the red shuttle/thread source) can be tatted first/second. One way to create this split ring is to use the red shuttle/thread source to tat 10 regular, transferred double stitches. Then use the green shuttle/thread source to tat 10 reverse, untransferred double stitches. Close the ring by pulling the red shuttle/thread source.

Ring #3 is an uneven split ring (SR3) with two take-off rings associated with it (TOR4 & TOR5). These 3 rings (SR3, TOR4, & TOR5) are tatted as a unit in 6 steps:

    Step 1: With the green shuttle/thread source tat 5 regular, transferred double stitches. You know to use this shuttle/thread source because of the colored letter 'A' associated with this portion of the split ring.
    Step 2: With the red shuttle/thread source tat 5 reverse, untransferred double stitches.
    Step 3: Take Split Ring 3 off your hand. Reverse work. With the red shuttle/thread tat Take Off Ring 4 as a regular ring of 20 transferrred double stitches. Close Take Off Ring 4. Reverse work.
    Step 4: Put Split Ring 3 back onto your hand. With the red shuttle thread source tat 5 more reverse, untransferred double stitches.
    Step 5: Take Split Ring 3 off your hand. Reverse work. With the red shuttle/thread tat Take Off Ring 5 as a regular ring of 20 transferrred double stitches. Close Take Off Ring 5. Reverse work.
    Step 6: Put Split Ring 3 back onto your hand. With the red shuttle thread source tat 5 more reverse, untransferred double stitches. Close Split Ring 3 by pulling the green shuttle/thread source.

Ring #6 is a regular tatted ring. Only one shuttle/thread source is needed. Either thread source can be used. To follow the illustration, use the red shuttle/thread source to tat 20 regular, transferred double stitches, then close the ring.

Notes on direction of the arcs of the rings & their various portions and relationship to Frontside/Back Tatting Technique & Reverse Work:

 -- *R1: the red arc is clockwise--this is a 'frontside' ring.*

 -- *SR2: depend upon which shuttle/thread source is used first. If the red shuttle/thread source is used for the first step/portion of the split ring then the arc is clockwise, thus it is a 'frontside' ring. Both portions are tatted the same way--as 'frontside' stitches. However, if the green shuttle/thread source is used first, the arc of this portion is counter-clockwise, thus the entire split ring would be tatted as a 'backside' ring.*

 -- *SR3 directs you to tat the green shuttle/thread source first. Since this arc is counter-clockwise the entire split ring would be tatted as a 'backside' ring.*

 -- *TOR4, TOR5, & R6 are all clockwise & thus are 'frontside' rings using the red shuttle/thread source.*

 -- *Because SR3 is a 'backside' ring and then TOR 4/5 are 'frontside' rings, you will need to Reverse Work when going from SR3 to TOR4 (Same for SR3 to TOR5). Another Reverse Work is needed when going from SR3 (a 'backside' ring) to R6 (a 'frontside' ring).*

APPROACH TO WORKING PATCHWORK QUILT BLOCK PATTERNS

Quilt-Inspired Split Ring Tatting patterns like historic, fabric quilts have symmetry. Instead of every patchwork block being a separate pattern, the following patterns are constructed usually from the center outward. The patchwork block design is tatted in 'rounds' as directed by the numbers. Each separate block/round has a number. Start tatting block #1, then block #2, & so on. Blocks of the same size/shape/attachment will have the same pattern. These patterns are designated by the capital letters. This approach is taken to simplify the pattern process as well as minimize the number of patterns needed. If each block had its own pattern this book would be much larger or feature fewer patterns.

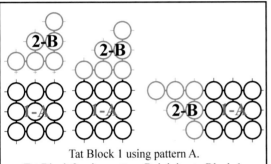

Tat Block 1 using pattern A.
Tat Block 2 using pattern B, joining to Block 1.
Turn *(not reverse work)* the piece
90 degrees counter-clockwise.

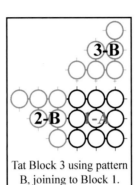

Tat Block 3 using pattern
B, joining to Block 1.

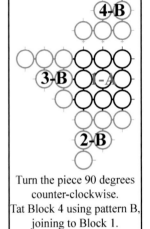

Turn the piece 90 degrees
counter-clockwise.
Tat Block 4 using pattern B,
joining to Block 1.

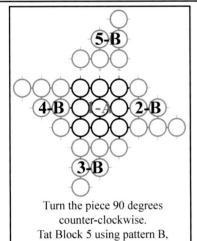

Turn the piece 90 degrees
counter-clockwise.
Tat Block 5 using pattern B,
joining to Block 1.

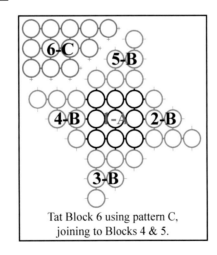

Tat Block 6 using pattern C,
joining to Blocks 4 & 5.

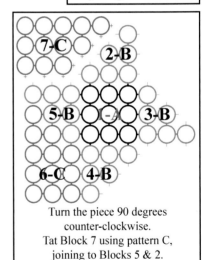

Turn the piece 90 degrees
counter-clockwise.
Tat Block 7 using pattern C,
joining to Blocks 5 & 2.

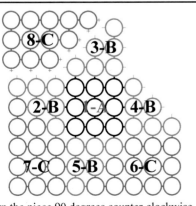

Turn the piece 90 degrees counter-clockwise.
Tat Block 8 using pattern C, joining to Blocks 2 & 3.

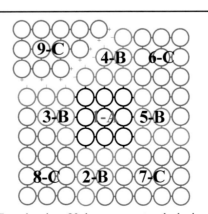

Turn the piece 90 degrees counter-clockwise.
Tat Block 9 using pattern C, joining to Blocks 3 & 4.

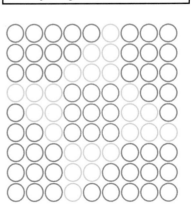

7

Wreath

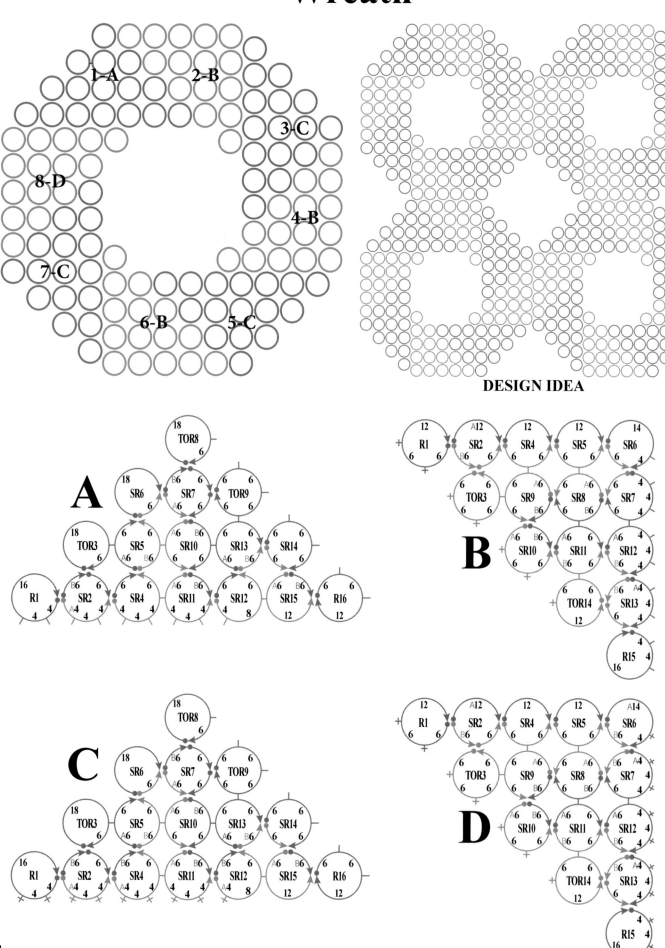

DESIGN IDEA

8

Eight Pointed Star

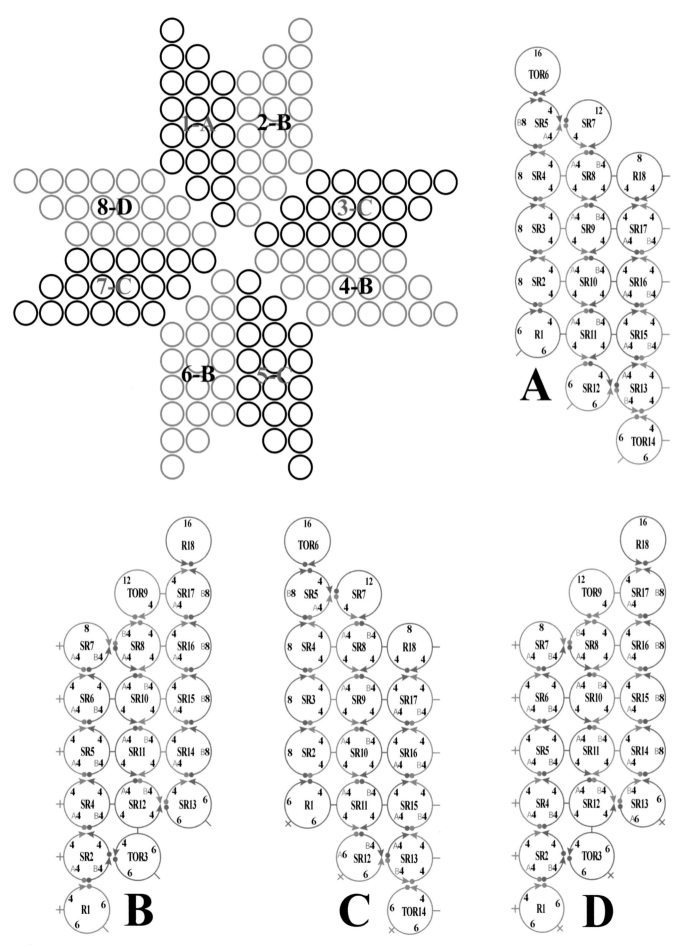

Card Trick

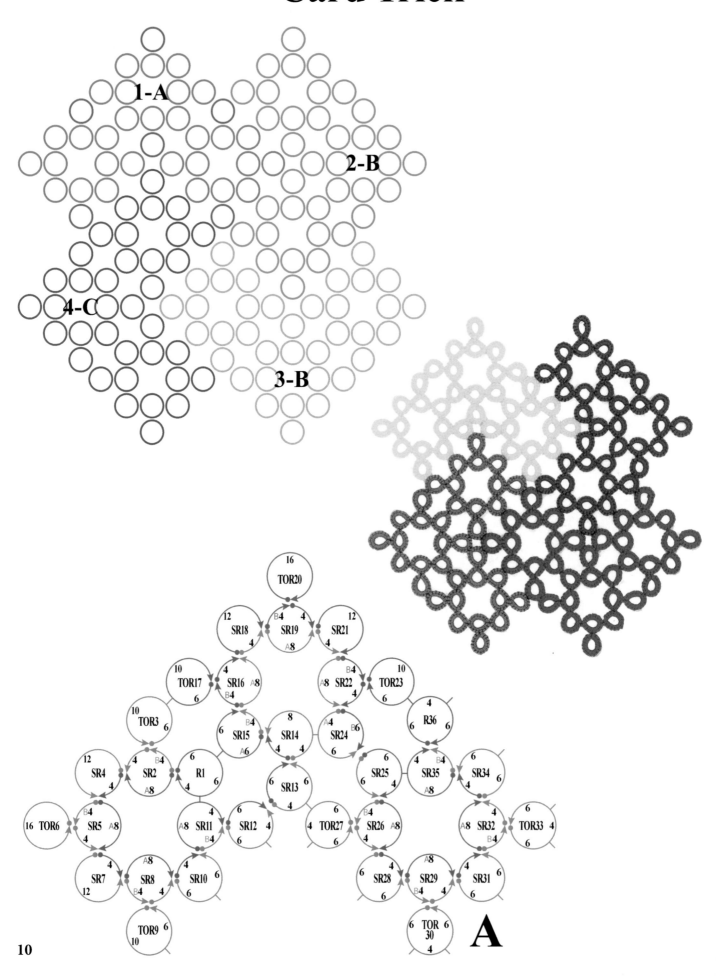

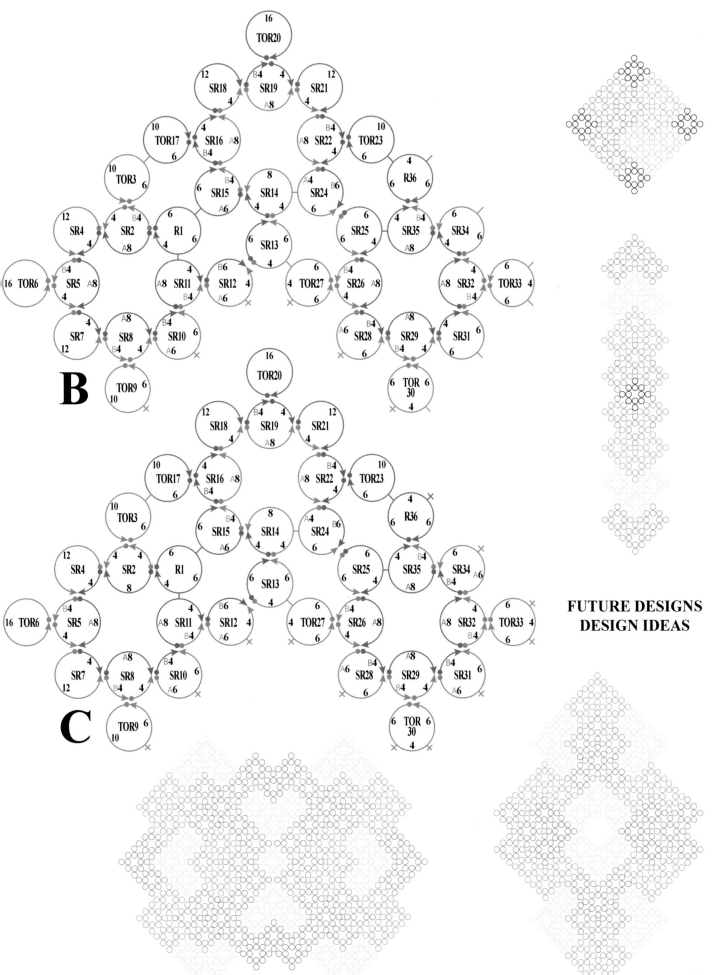

B

C

**FUTURE DESIGNS
DESIGN IDEAS**

Quilted Heart

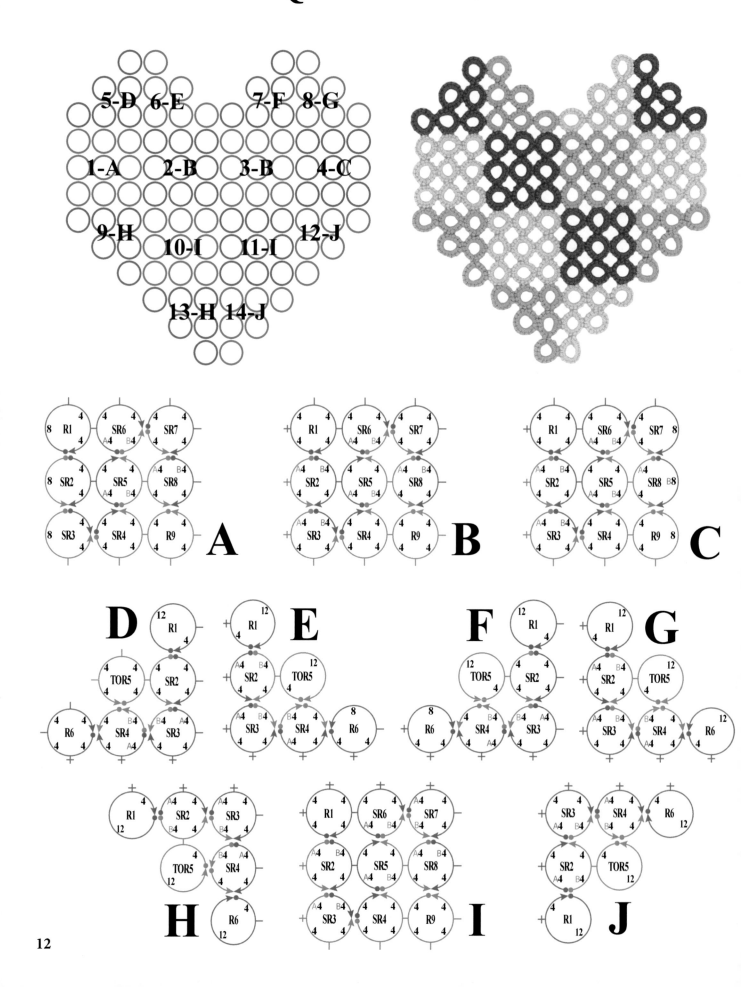

Granny Square

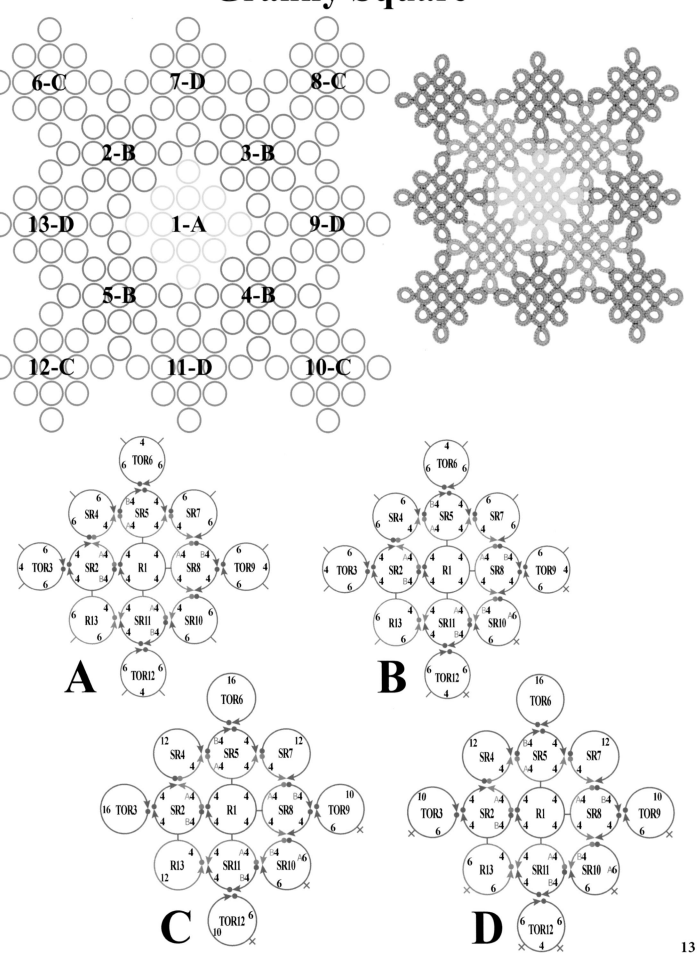

6-C 7-D 8-C

2-B 3-B

13-D 1-A 9-D

5-B 4-B

12-C 11-D 10-C

A

TOR6
SR4 SR5 SR7
TOR3 SR2 R1 SR8 TOR9
R13 SR11 SR10
TOR12

B

TOR6
SR4 SR5 SR7
TOR3 SR2 R1 SR8 TOR9
R13 SR11 SR10
TOR12

C

TOR6
SR4 SR5 SR7
TOR3 SR2 R1 SR8 TOR9
R13 SR11 SR10
TOR12

D

TOR6
SR4 SR5 SR7
TOR3 SR2 R1 SR8 TOR9
R13 SR11 SR10
TOR12

13

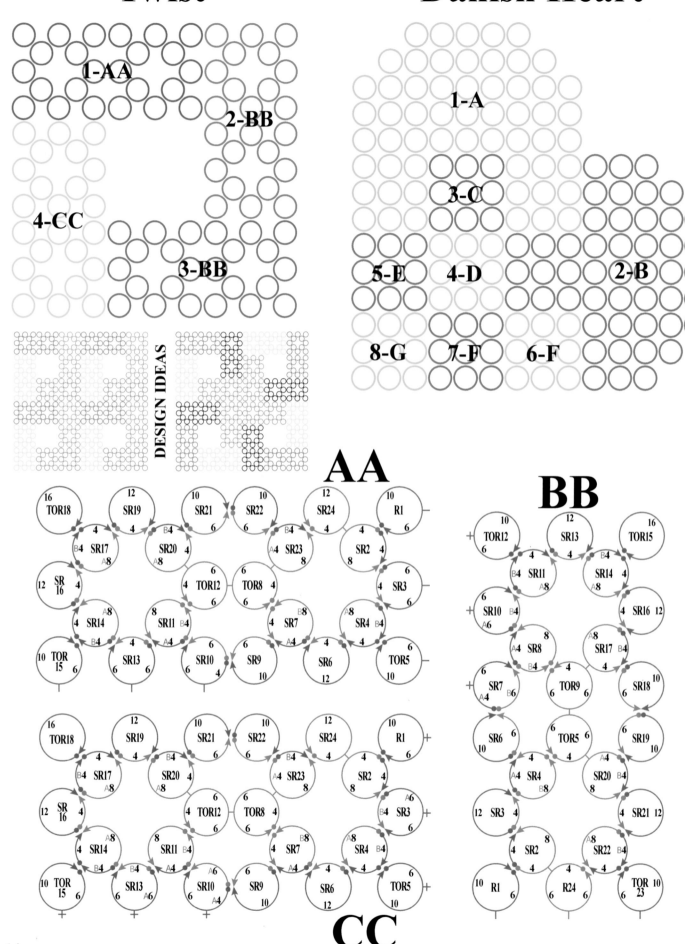

Twist

1-AA

2-BB

4-CC

3-BB

DESIGN IDEAS

Danish Heart

1-A

3-C

5-E   4-D   2-B

8-G   7-F   6-F

AA

BB

CC

14

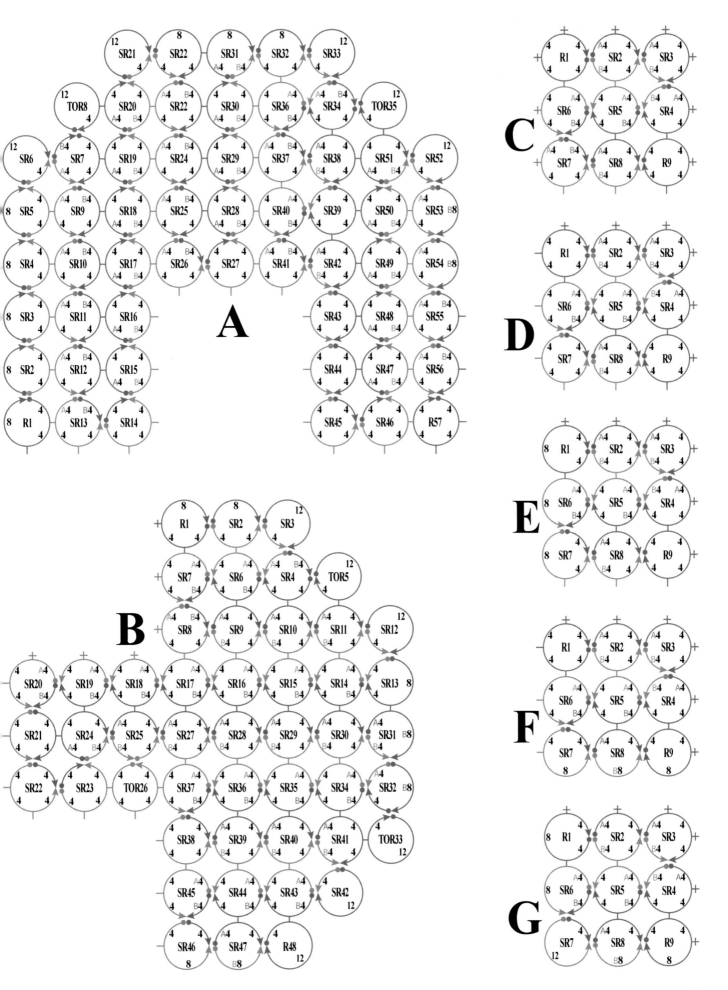

Sienna Square

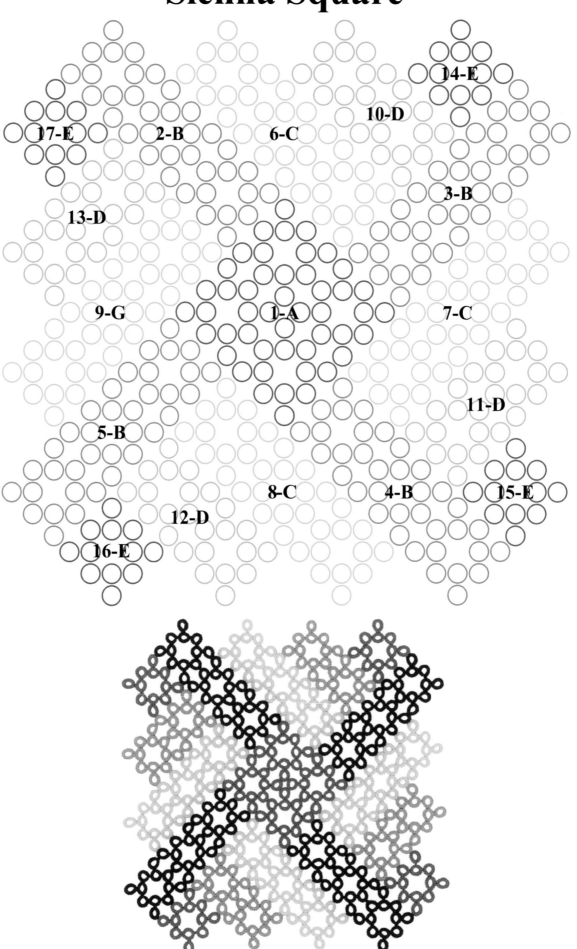

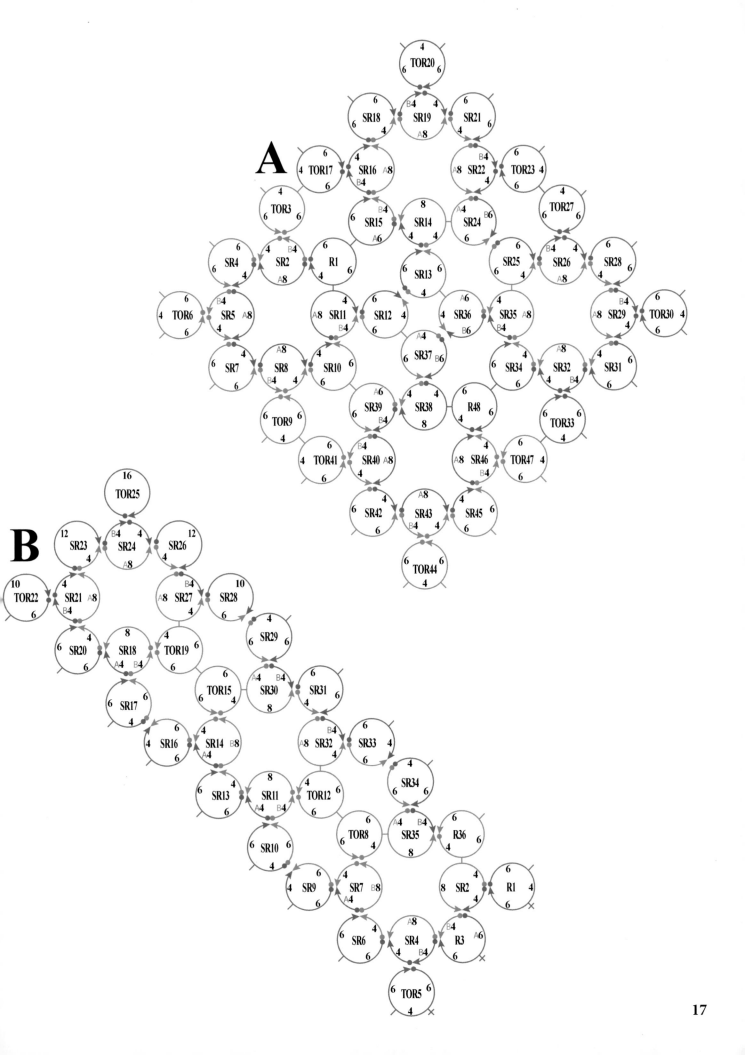

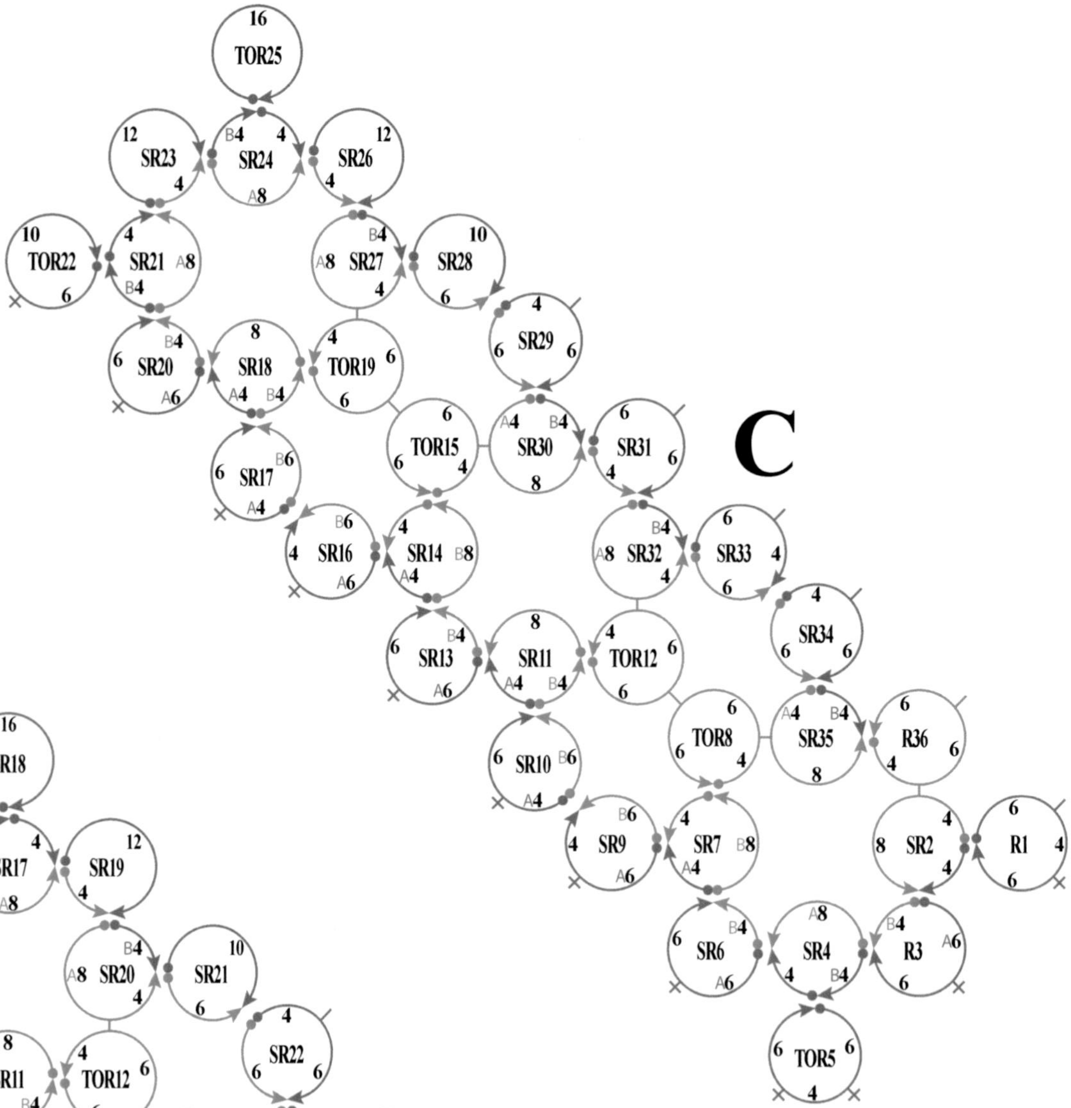
TOR25
SR23
SR24
SR26
TOR22
SR21
SR27
SR28
SR20
SR18
TOR19
SR29
SR17
TOR15
SR30
SR31
SR16
SR14
SR32
SR33
SR13
SR11
TOR12
SR34
SR10
TOR8
SR35
R36
SR9
SR7
SR2
R1
SR6
SR4
R3
TOR5

C

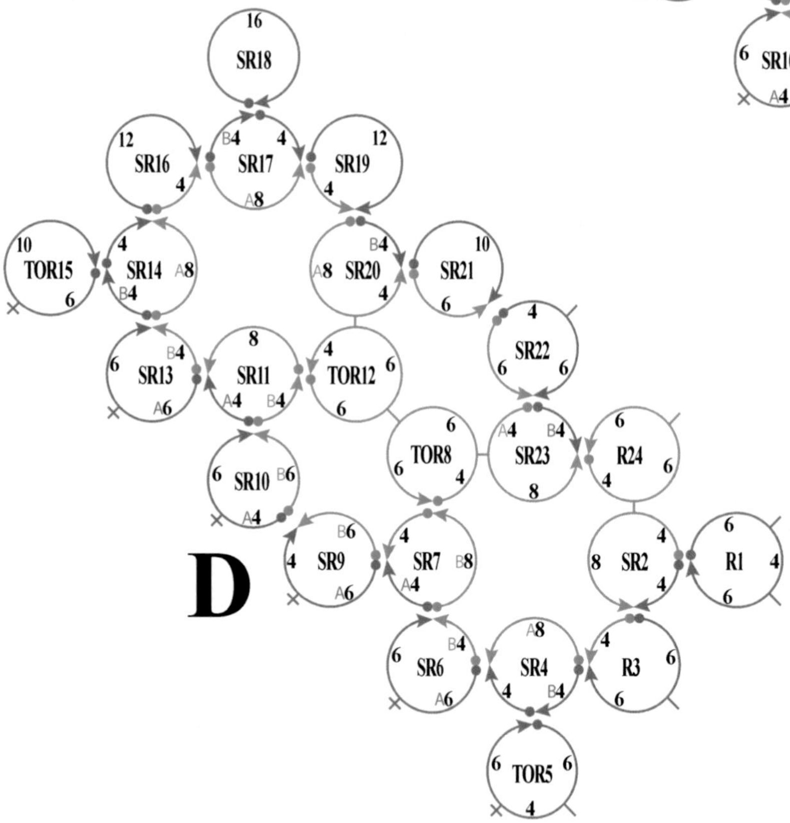
SR18
SR16
SR17
SR19
TOR15
SR14
SR20
SR21
SR13
SR11
TOR12
SR22
SR10
TOR8
SR23
R24
SR9
SR7
SR2
R1
SR6
SR4
R3
TOR5

D

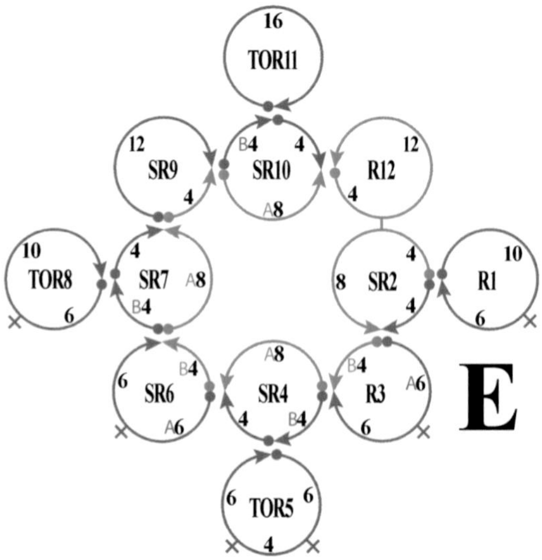
TOR11
SR9
SR10
R12
TOR8
SR7
SR2
R1
SR6
SR4
R3
TOR5

E

Woven Ribbons

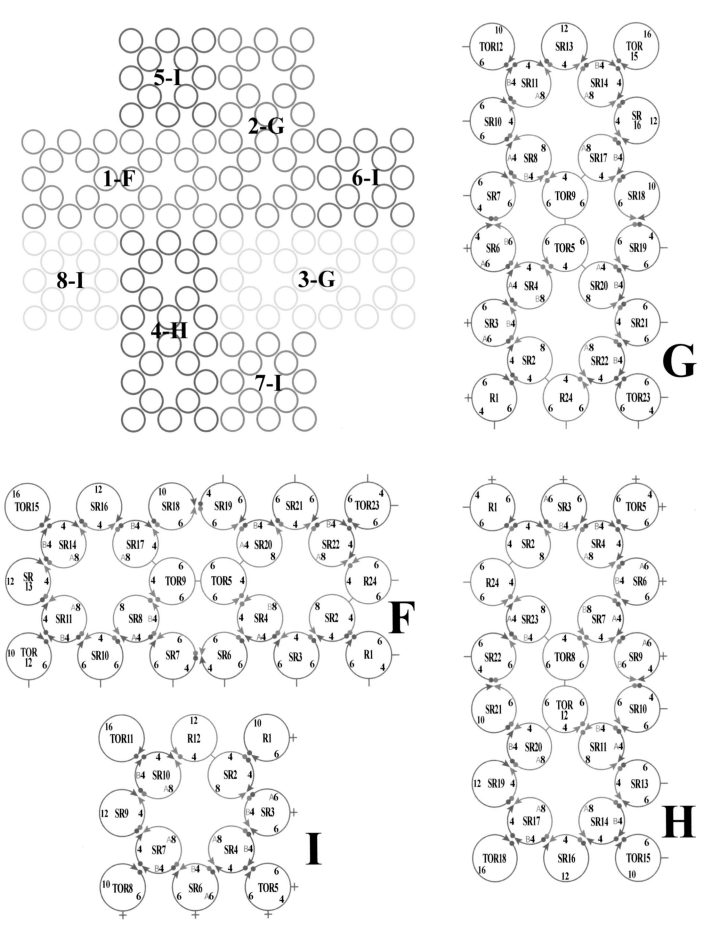

19

Dominos & Squares

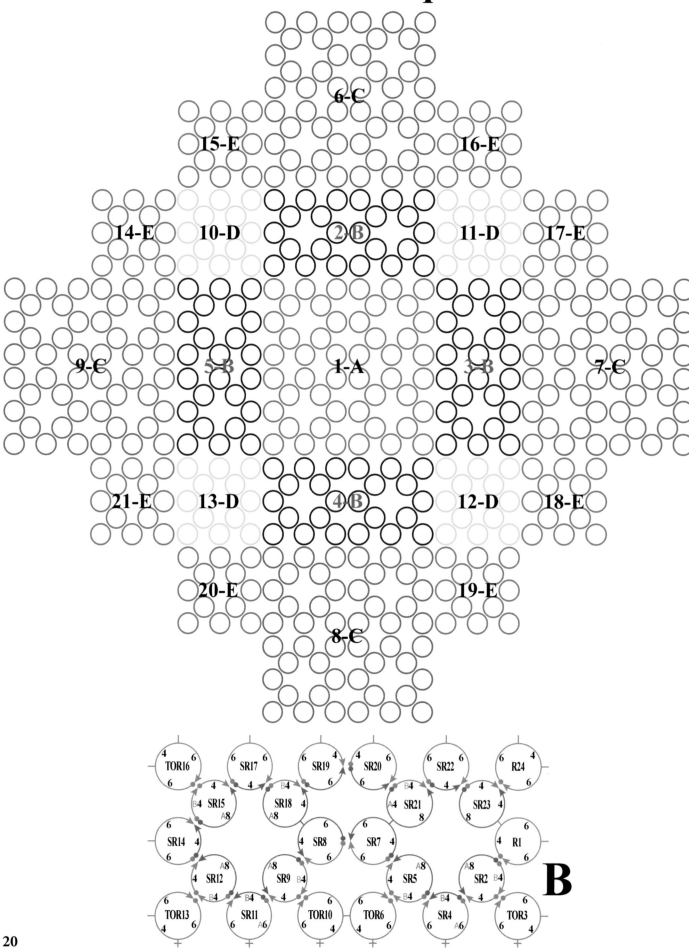

6-C

15-E 16-E

14-E 10-D 2-B 11-D 17-E

9-C 5-B 1-A 3-B 7-C

21-E 13-D 4-B 12-D 18-E

20-E 19-E

8-C

B

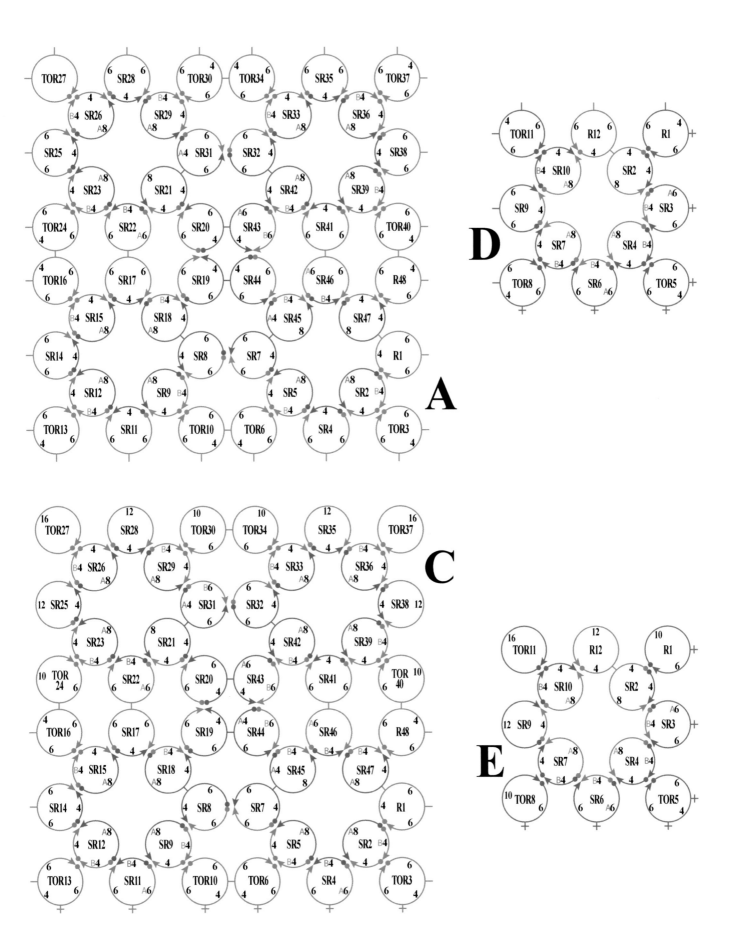

Log Cabin

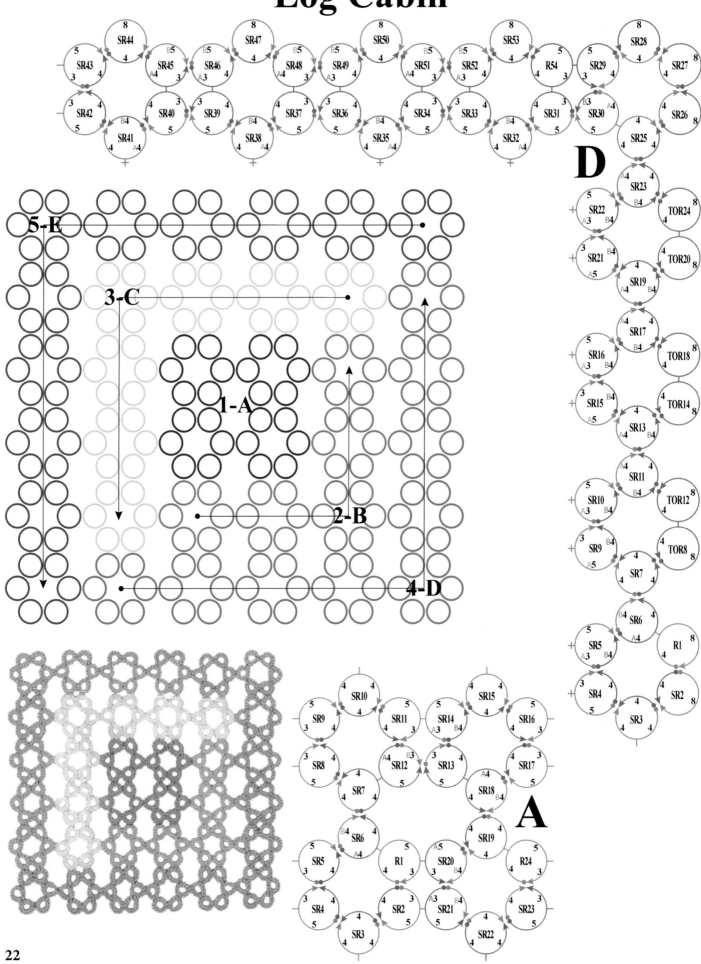

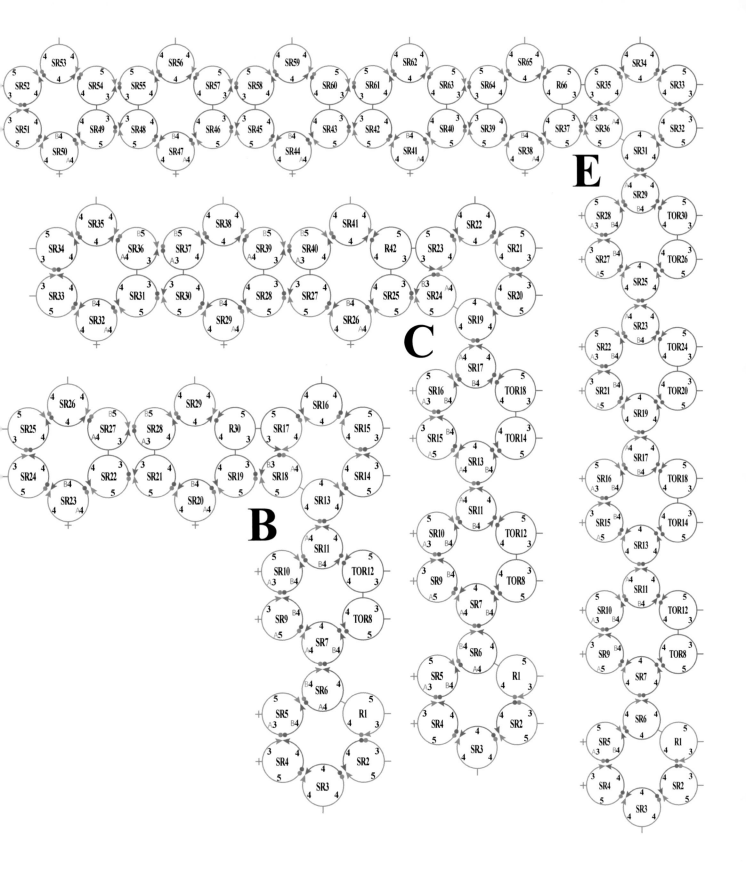

Flying Geese

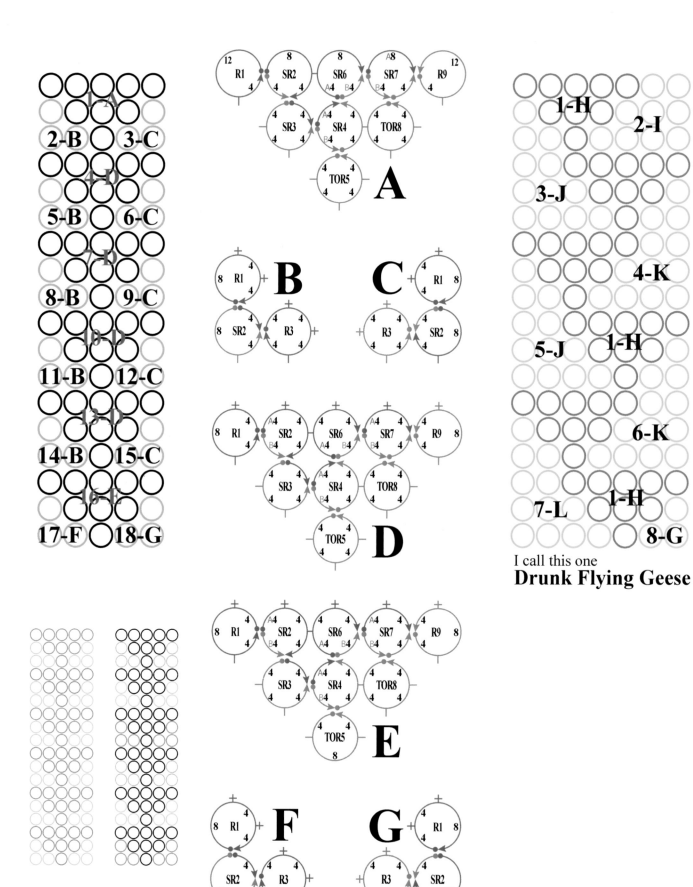

I call this one
Drunk Flying Geese

24

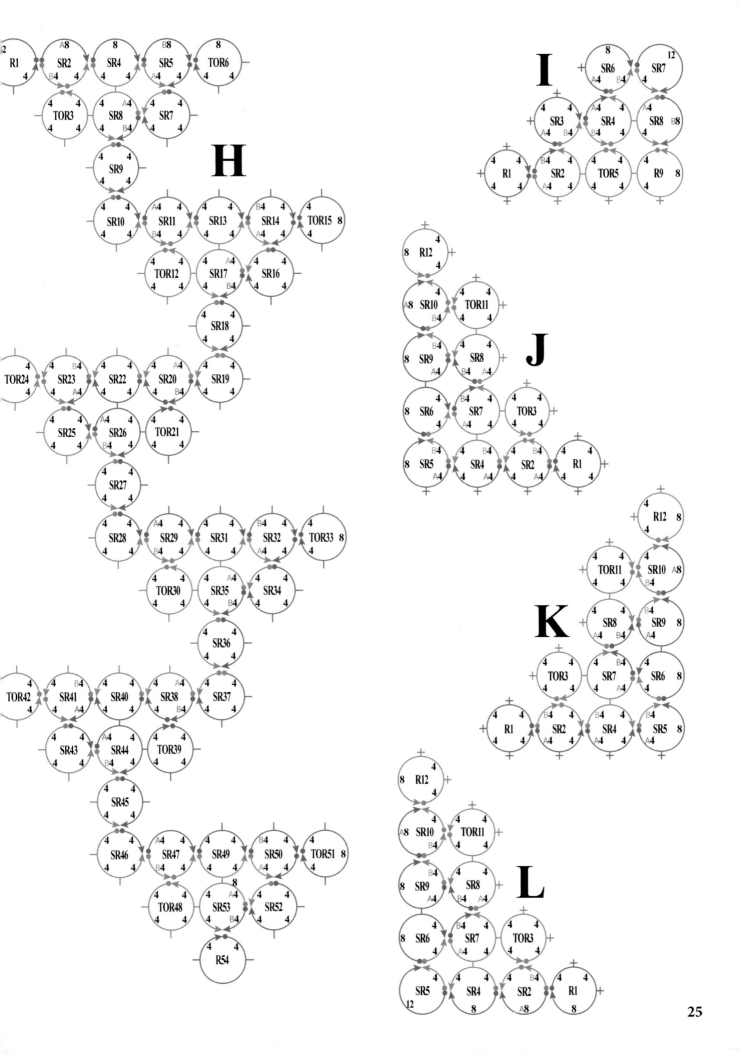

25

Flying Geese in Opposite Directions

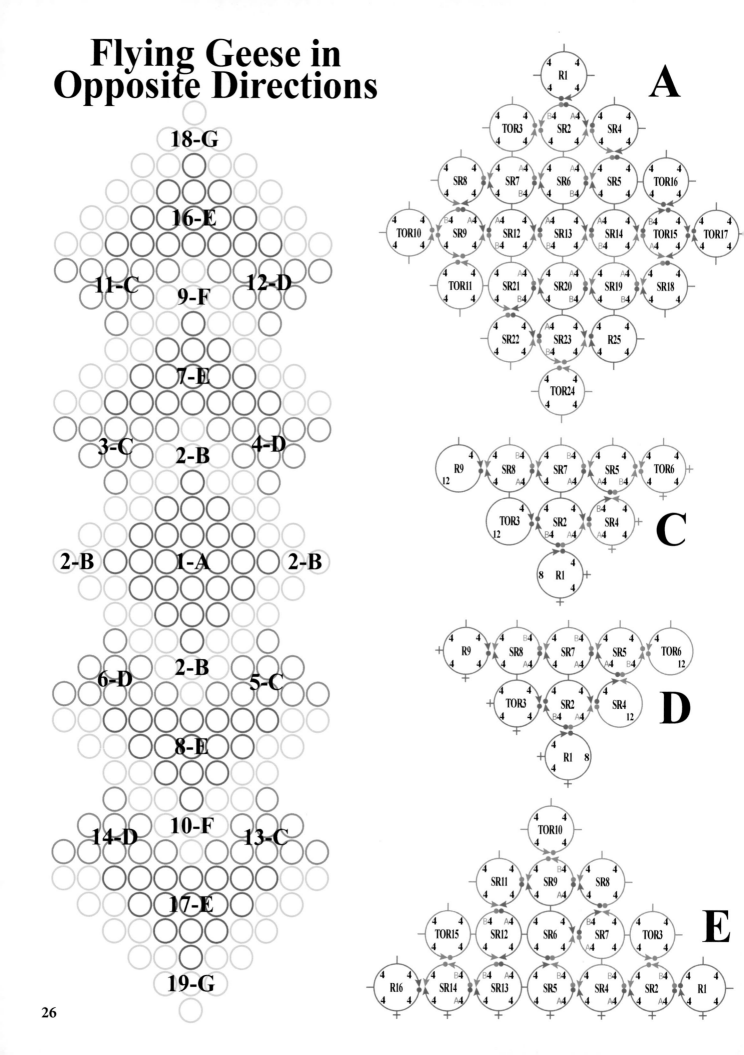

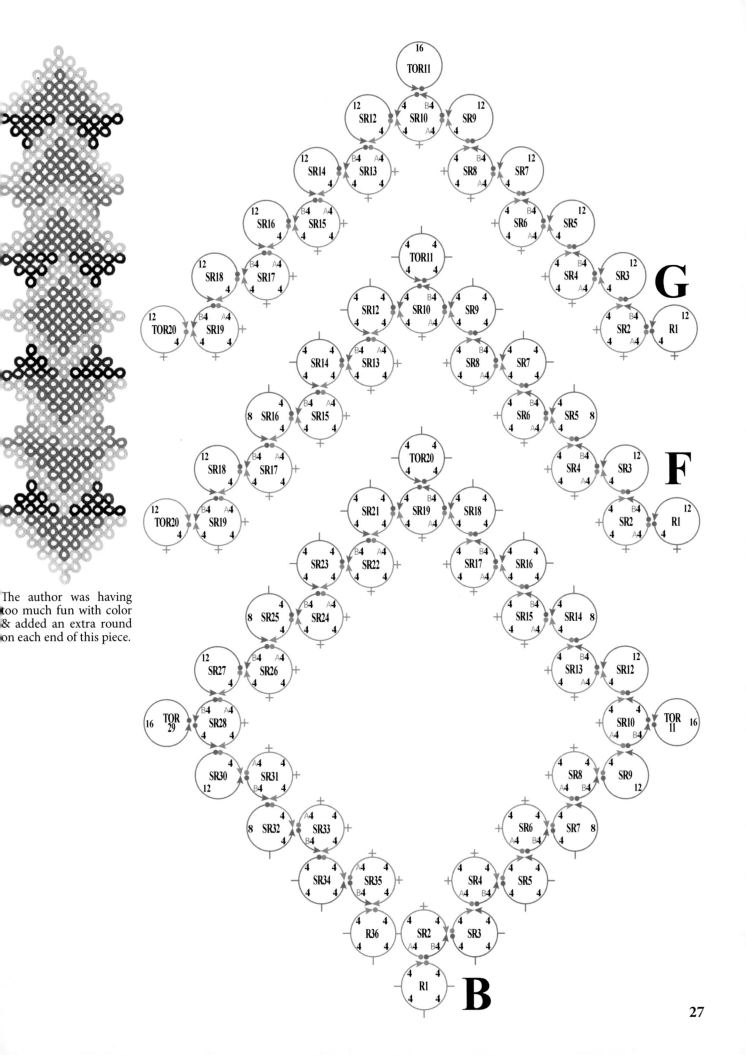

The author was having too much fun with color & added an extra round on each end of this piece.

G

F

B

Diamond-Based

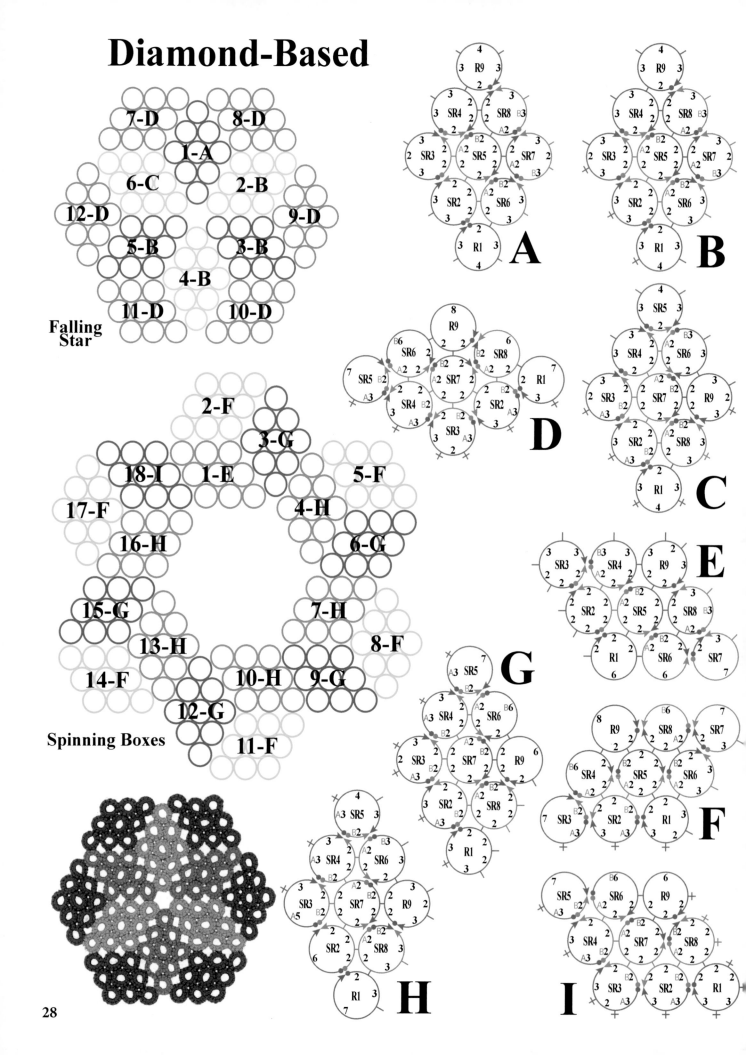

Falling Star

7-D   8-D
1-A
6-C   2-B
12-D   9-D
5-B   3-B
4-B
11-D   10-D

Spinning Boxes

2-F
3-G
18-I   1-E
17-F   5-F
4-H
16-H
6-G
15-G
7-H
13-H
14-F   8-F
10-H   9-G
12-G
11-F

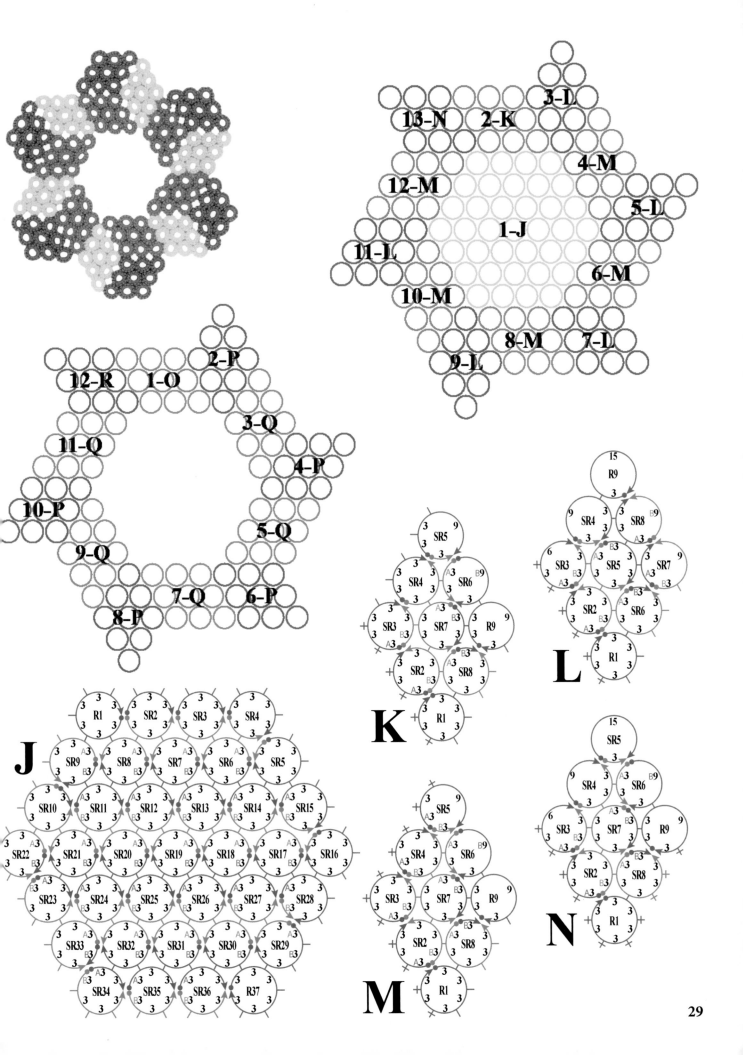

29

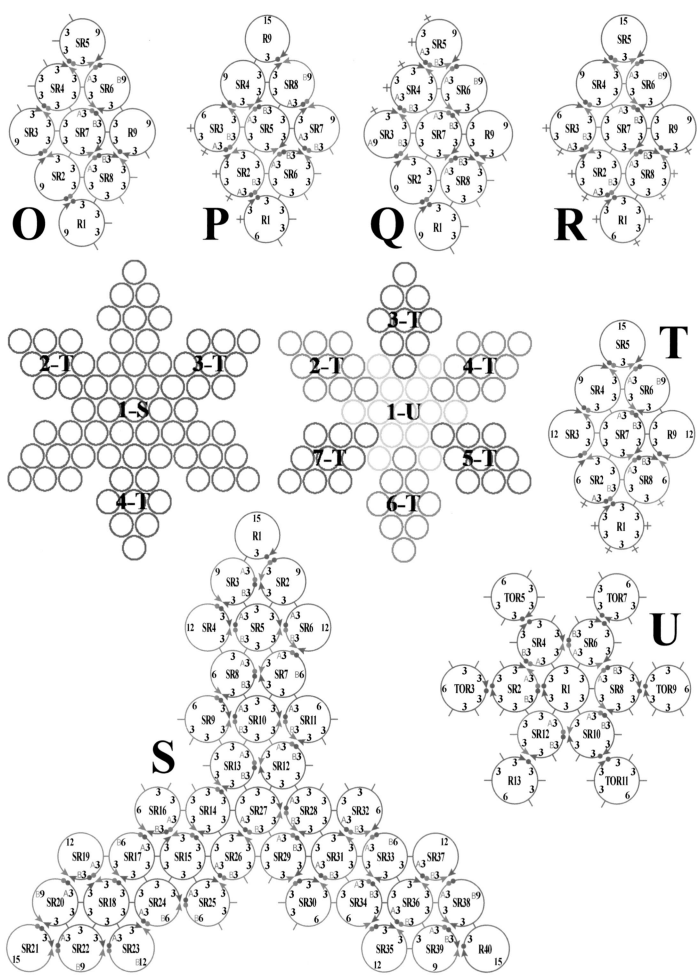

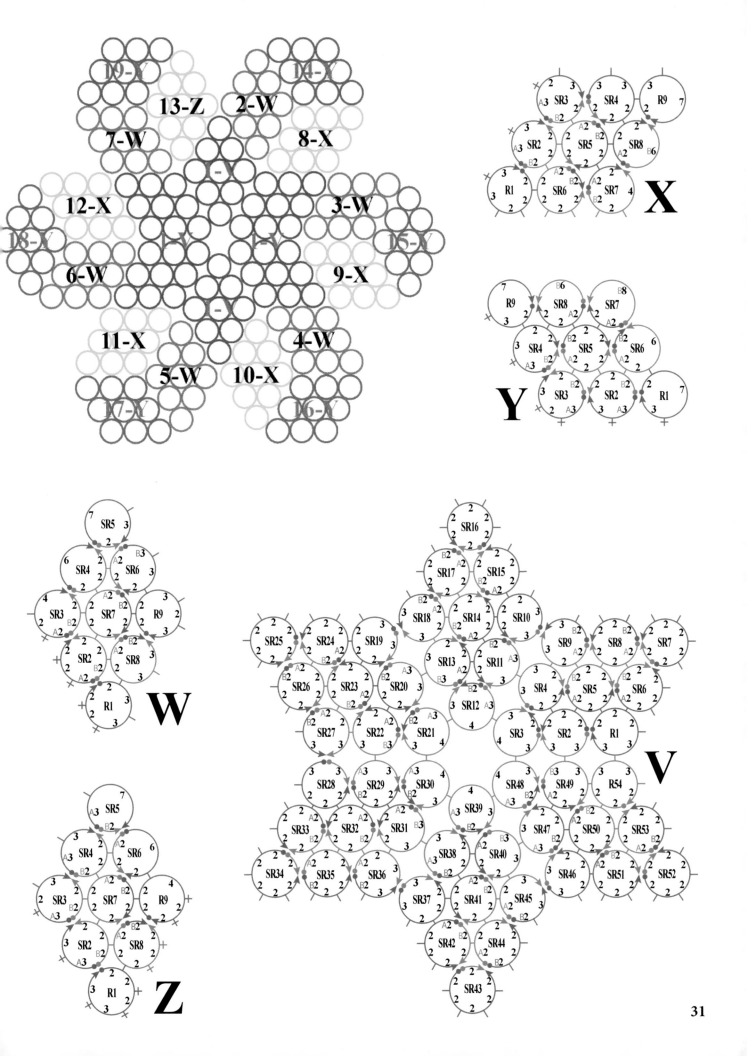

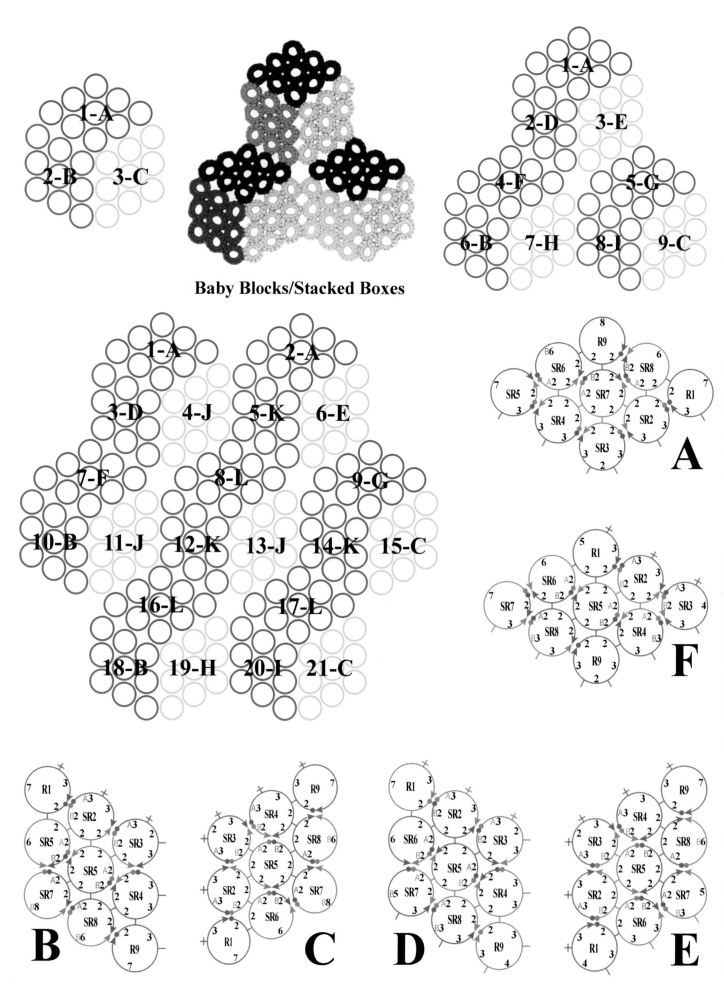

Baby Blocks/Stacked Boxes

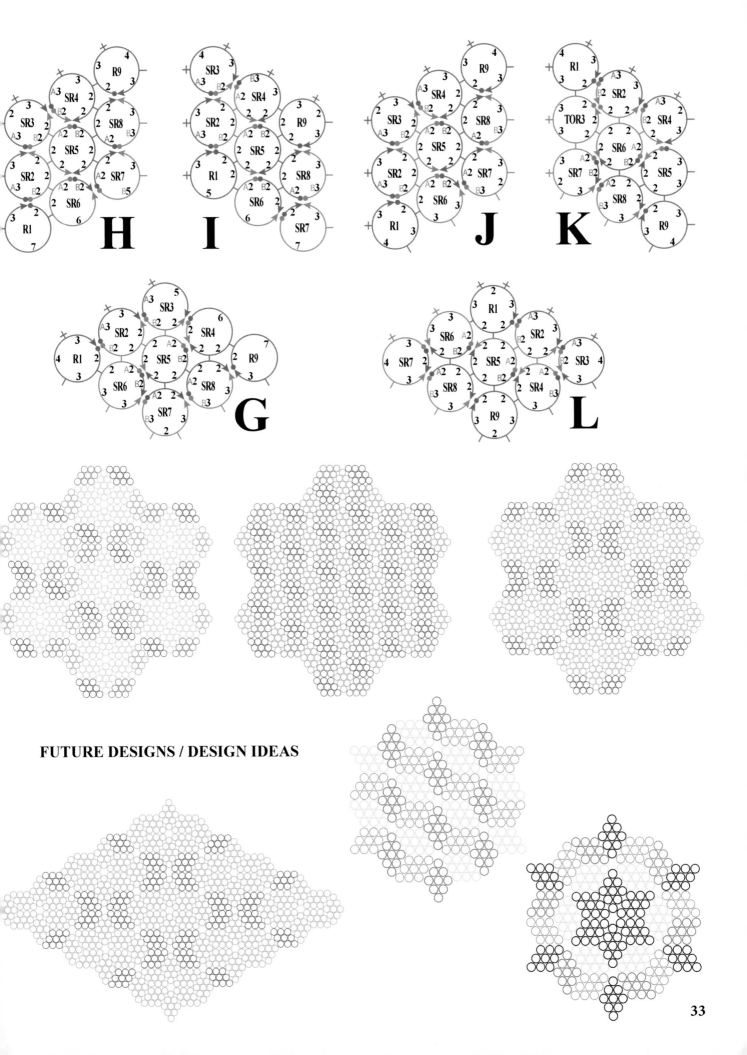

FUTURE DESIGNS / DESIGN IDEAS

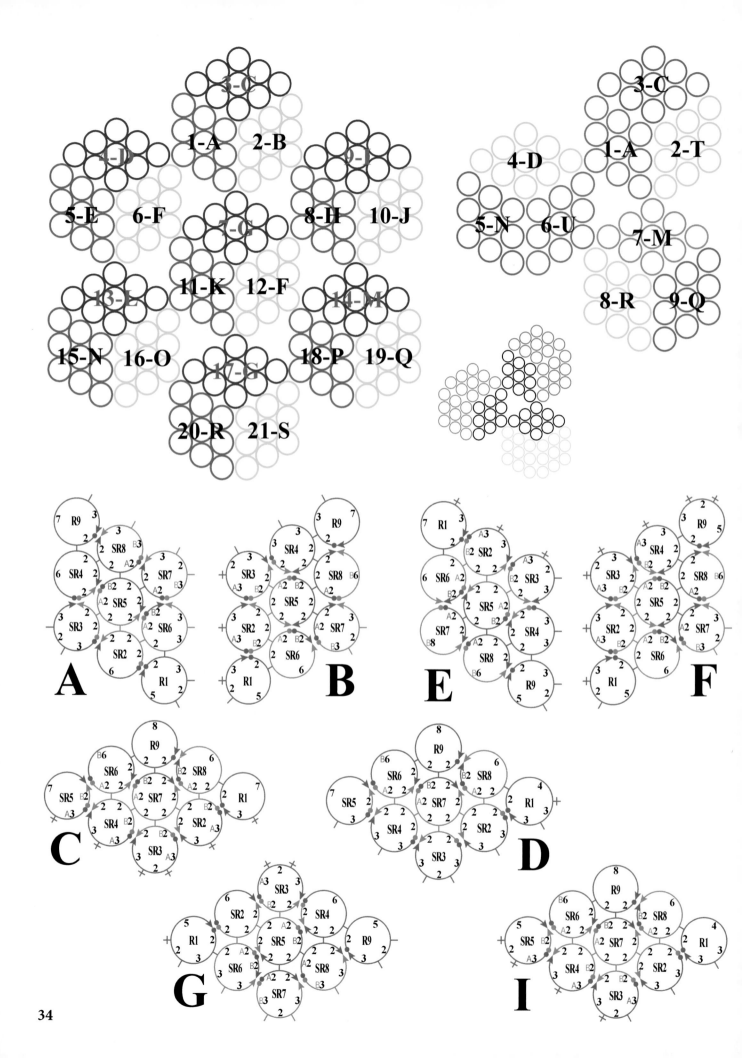

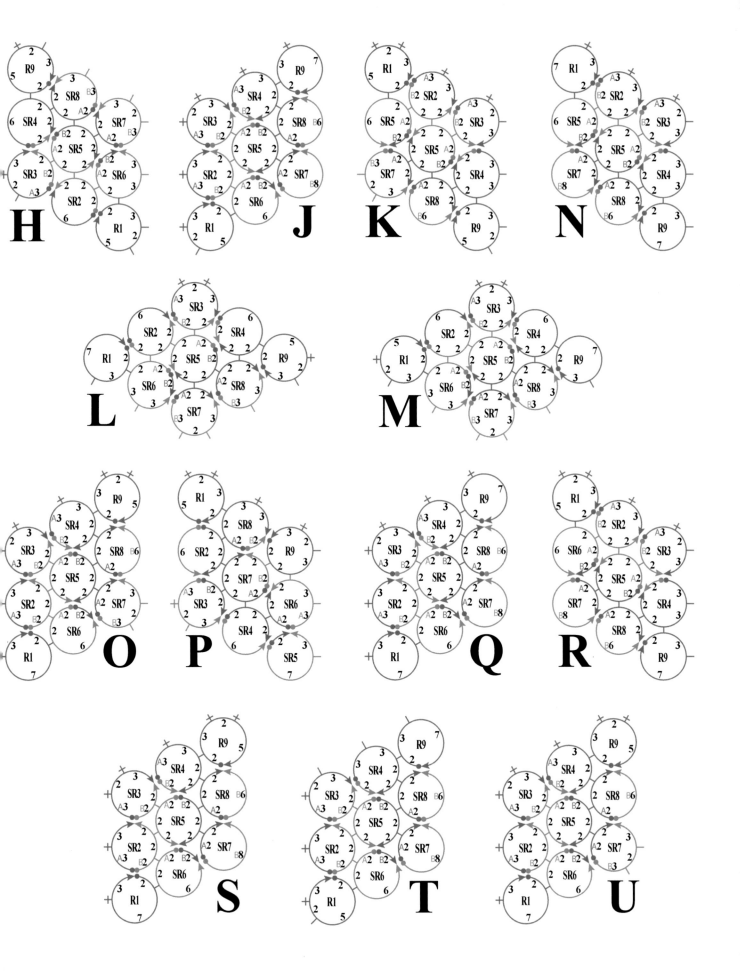

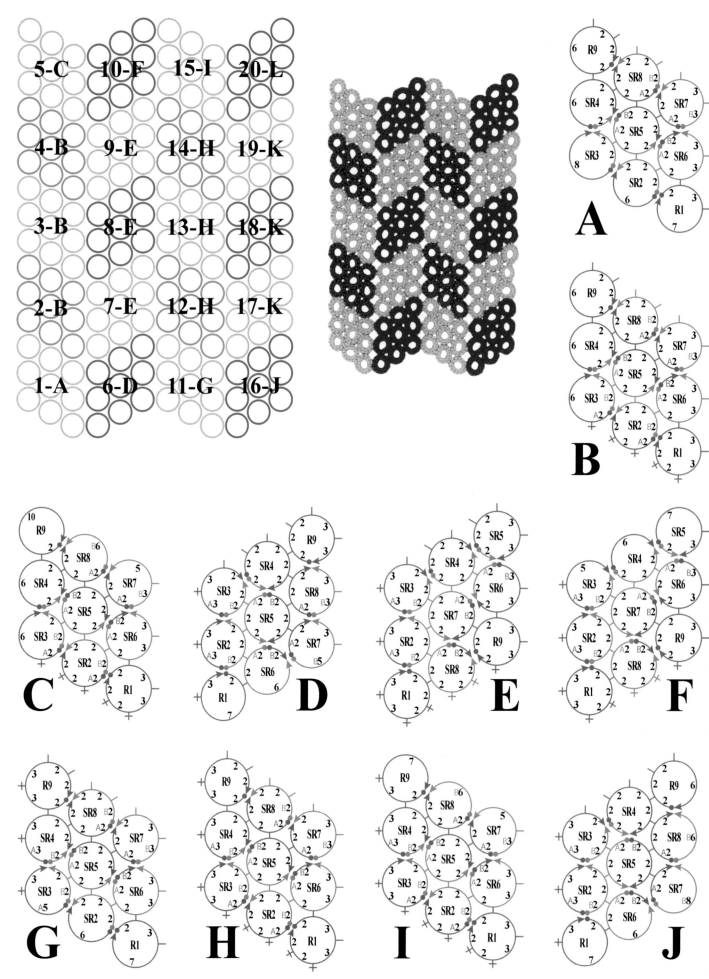

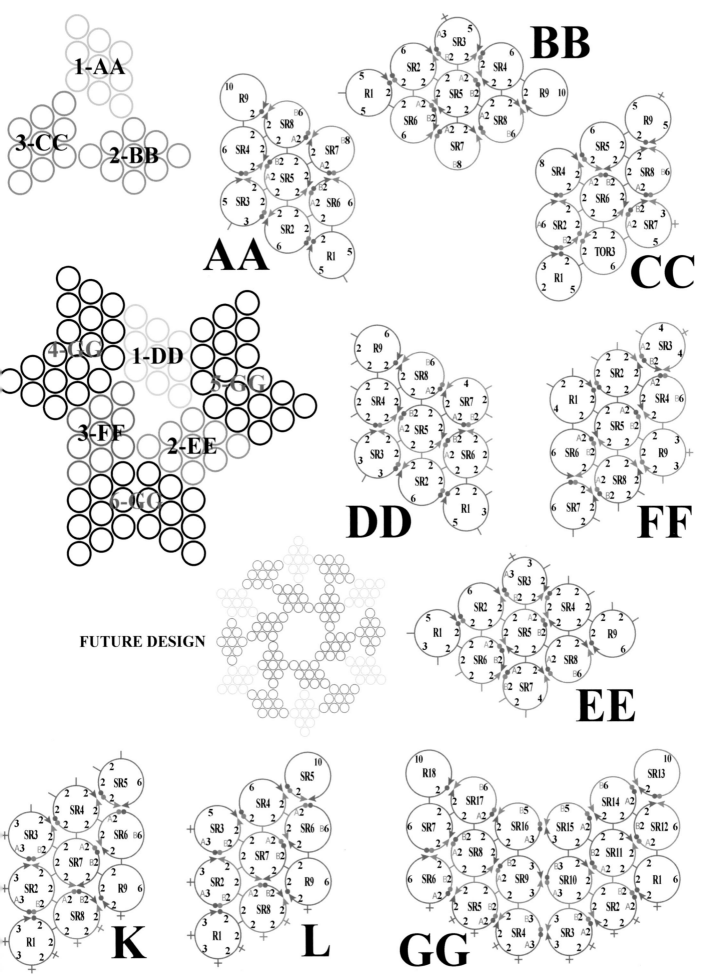

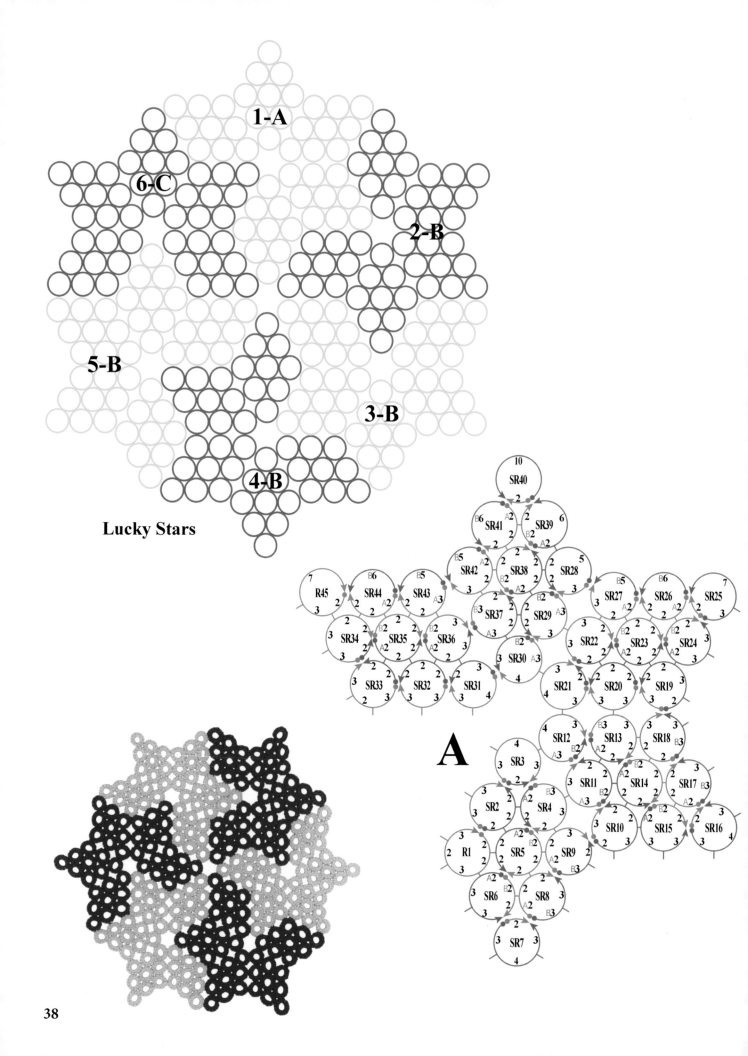

1-A

6-C

2-B

5-B

3-B

4-B

Lucky Stars

A

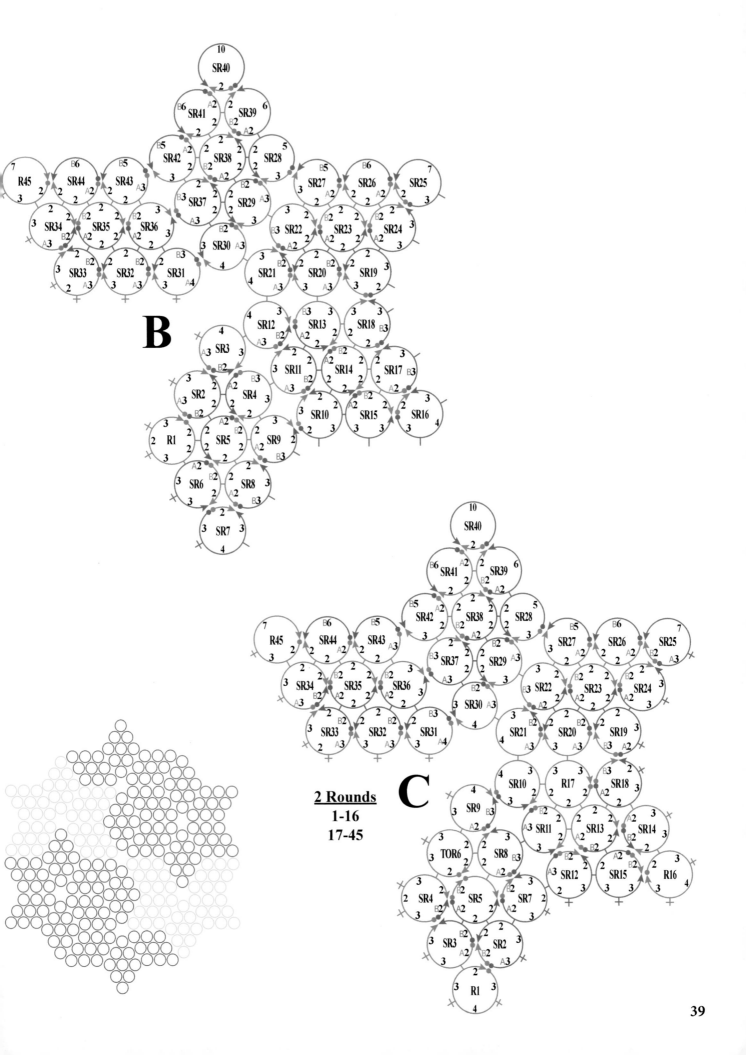

B

C

2 Rounds
1-16
17-45

Grandmothers Flower Garden

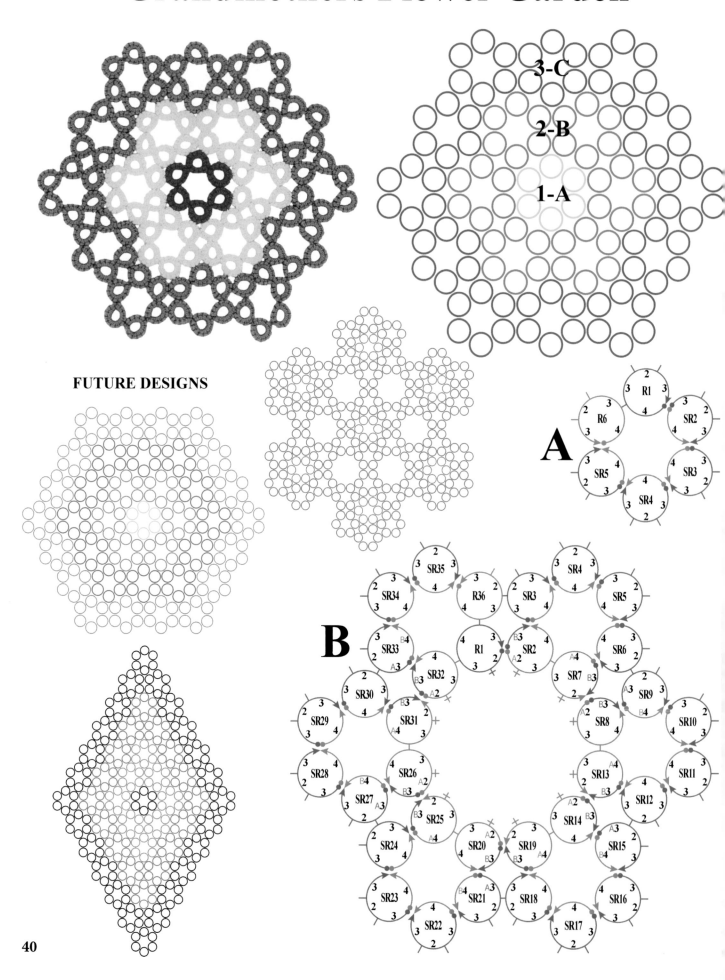

3-C

2-B

1-A

FUTURE DESIGNS

A

B

40

FUTURE DESIGNS

C

Pinwheel-Based

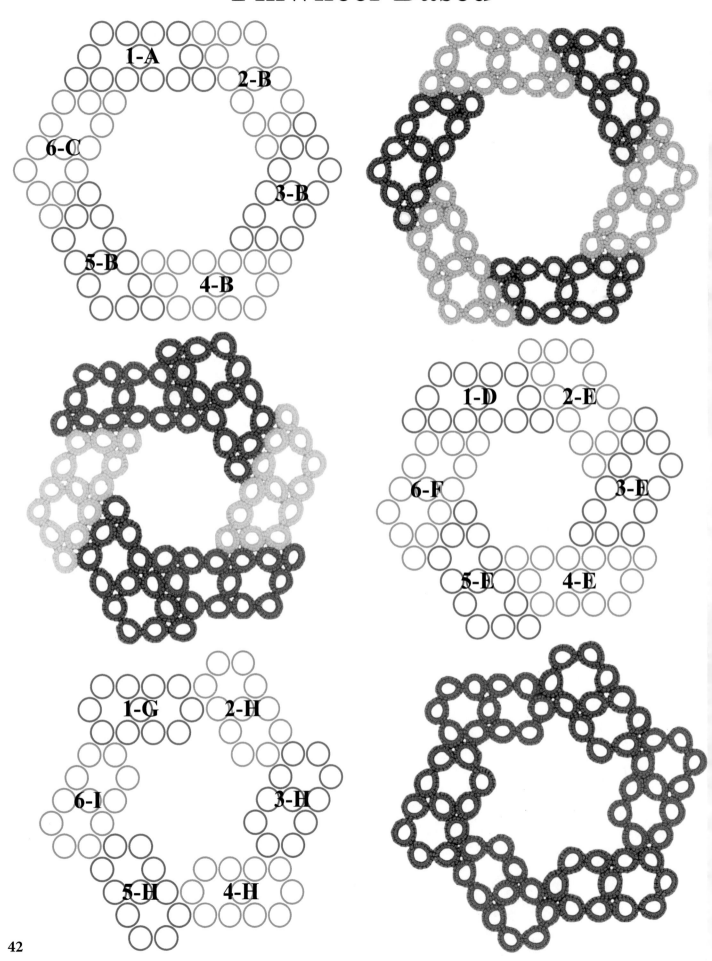

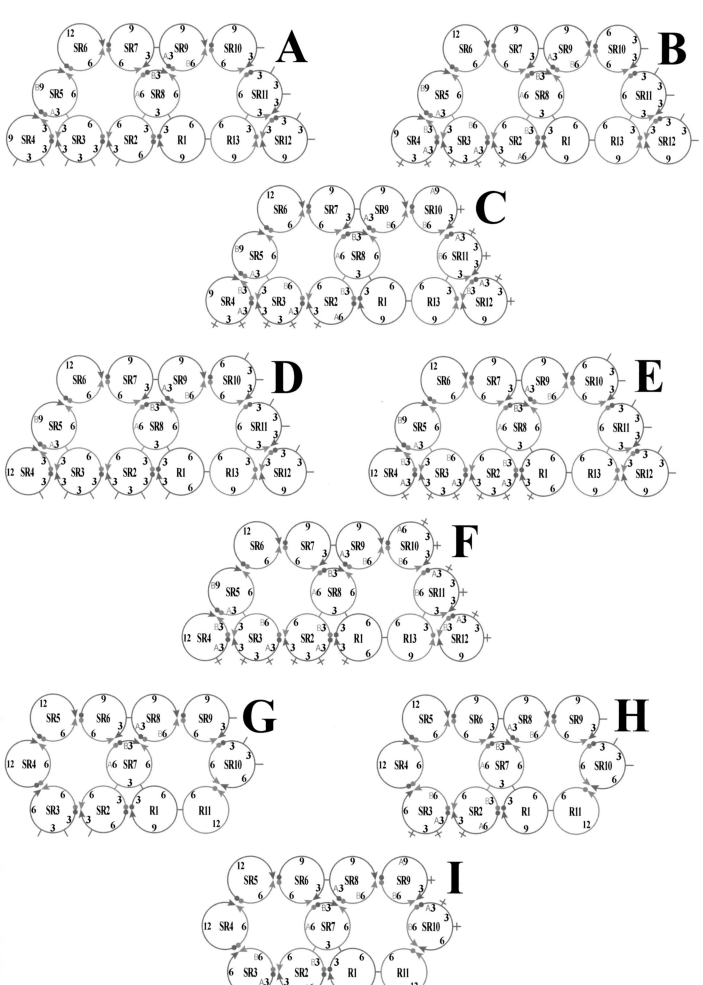

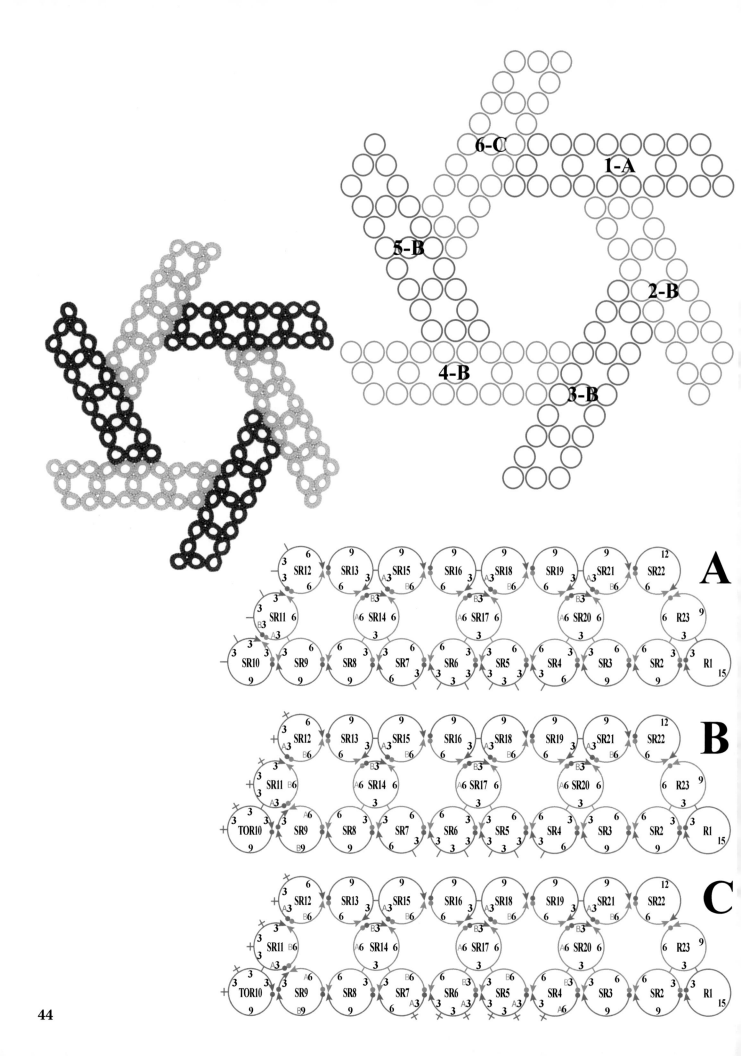

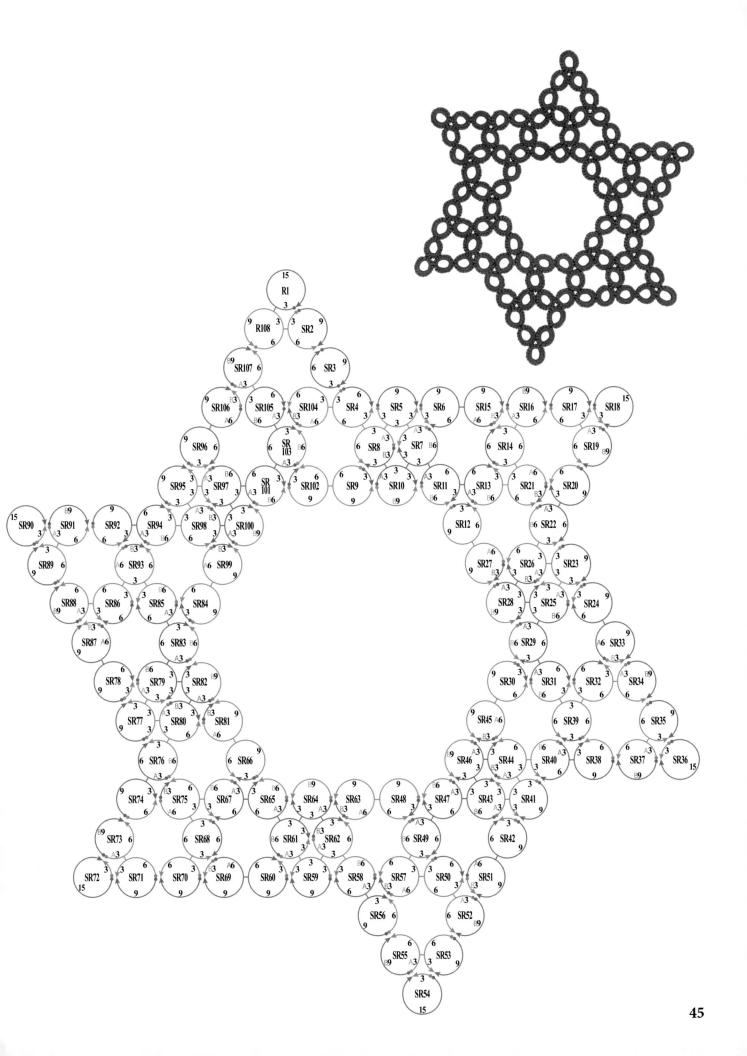

45

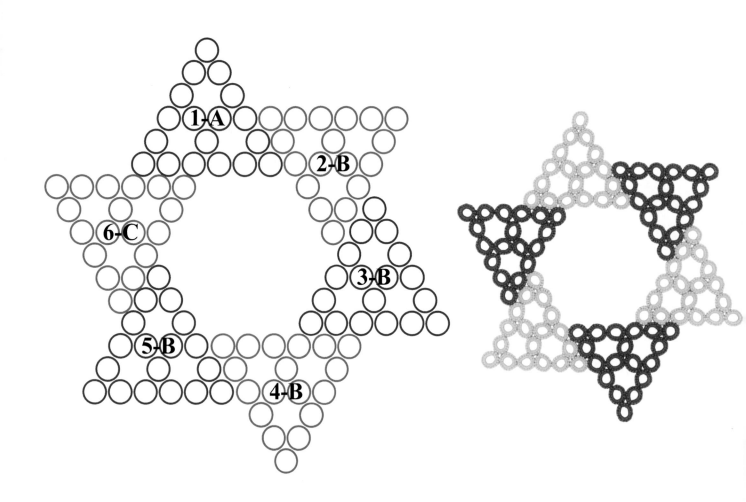

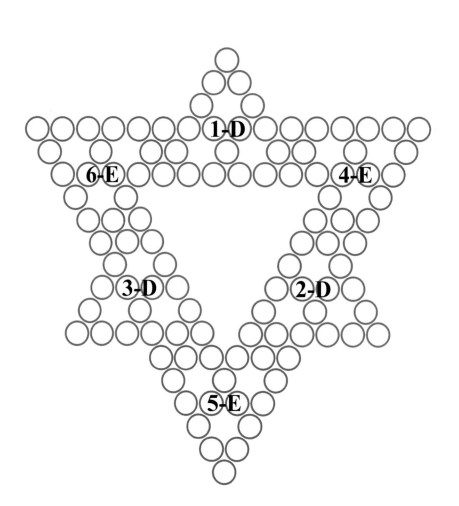

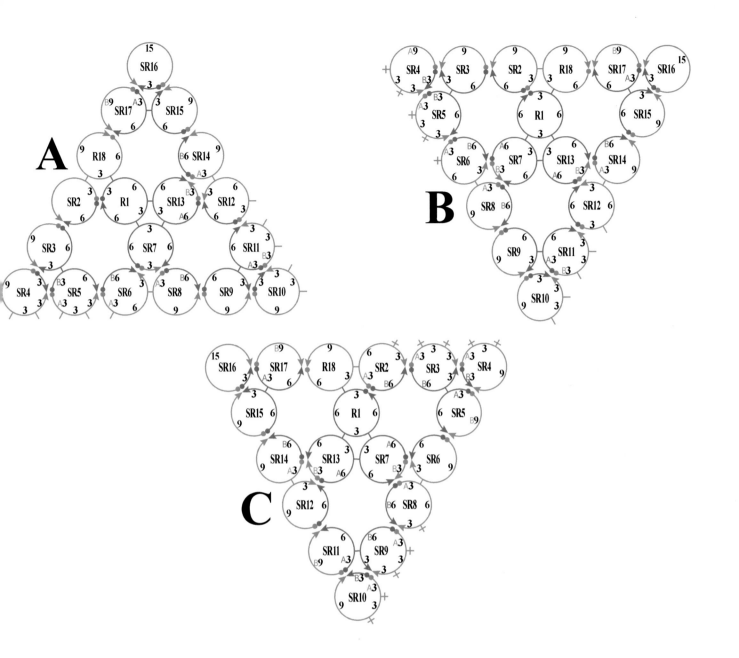

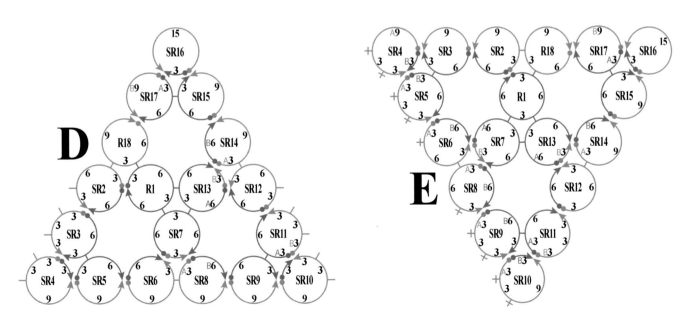

Made in the USA
Middletown, DE
24 February 2017